How to Keep Your Parish Alive

Eileen McCafferty DiFranco

ISBN-10:0-9969285-7-X
ISBN-13:978-0-9969285-7-1

Library of Congress Control Number: 2017952402

Published by Emergence Education Press
PO Box 63767
Philadelphia, PA 19147

www.EmergenceEducation.com

Dedicated to my grandchildren, Mark, Isabella, Amelia, and Windsor Mae, that their world will be filled with light and hope.

Acknowledgements

No one makes their life's journey alone. I'd like to thank my husband of forty-three years, Larry DiFranco, for his unfailing support of all of my ventures. I'd also like to thank my four children, Janine, Neil, Gregory, and Benjamin, who put up with my endless years in seminary and my many hours of writing theological tomes. My church home, the Saint Mary Magdalene Community, has also been a source of both inspiration and support.

I would also like to thank my former parish, St. Vincent de Paul in Philadelphia. St. Vincent's was the first parish I ever attended that taught that Catholics were actually obliged to follow the gospel message of Jesus to care for the sick, visit the imprisoned, feed the hungry, and work for justice. They did so by establishing a soup kitchen, a thrift store, a law clinic, and a nurses' clinic that served the poor. Going to church was not enough to define one's faith. We had to be a church for the world. Belonging to St. Vincent's changed my life. The late Bud Englert, a man of uncommon goodness, was the inspiration behind St. Vincent's transformation into a peace and justice parish. This book would have been impossible without Bud's presence, influence, and love.

CONTENTS

STATEMENT ABOUT
THE KINGDOM OF GOD

Many would eschew using the phrase "Kingdom of God" in a twenty-first-century book because it conveys the image of power rather than of peace and equality. I did the same until I read the late Marcus Borg's reflection on the Kingdom of God. Borg changed my mind..

Borg said that Jesus used the image of a kingdom because it was the only form of political organization that his followers would have understood. When Jesus placed God rather than the Roman emperor as the head of his notion of kingdom, his message became revolutionary and eventually led to his arrest, torture, and execution as a political criminal.

While I believe that we live more in a *"kin-dom"* than a kingdom, I have come to appreciate the revolutionary image that Jesus conveyed in his use of this term. And so, I will use Jesus' own words of the Kingdom of God throughout this book.

A Psalm of New Wine Skins

Comfortable and well-worn are my daily paths
   whose edges have grown gray
   with constant use.

My daily speech is a collection of old words
   worn down at the heels by repeated use.

My language and deeds, addicted to habit,
   prefer the taste of old wine,
   the feel of weathered skin.

Come and awaken me, Spirit of the new.

Come and refresh me, Creator of green life.

Come and inspire me, Risen Son,
   you who make all things new:
   I am too young to be dead,
   to be stagnant in spirit.

High are the walls that guard the old,
   the tried and secure ways of yesterday
   that protect me from the dreaded plague,
   the feared heresy of change.

For all change is a danger to the trusted order,
   the threadbare traditions that are maintained
   by the narrow ruts of rituals.

Yet how can an everlastingly new covenant
    retain its freshness and vitality
    without injections of the new,
    the daring, and the untried?

Come, O you who are ever-new,
    wrap my heart in new skin,
    ever flexible to be reformed by your Spirit.

Set my feet to fresh paths this day:
    inspire me to speak original and life-giving words
    and to creatively give shape to the new.

Come and teach me how to dance with delight
    whenever you send a new melody my way.

— Edward Hays, *Prayers for a Planetary Pilgrim*

PROLOGUE
SINGING A NEW SONG

*"It is a good example to turn over the
responsibility and leadership to others."*

—*Roberta Brunner*

After Vatican II, a breath of fresh air wafted through the staid
and sober Archdiocese of Philadelphia. In the late 1960s, the
Medical Mission Sisters in Philadelphia began holding vibrant,
faith-filled, and joyous Eucharistic celebrations at their mother-
house. Attendance at the well-planned, innovative liturgies boomed
as three hundred people from one hundred and nine families worshipped each Sunday at what came to be called the Community of
the Christian Spirit (CCS).

The sisters set the stage for the implementation of a democratic
church. Lay leadership planned the liturgy, religious education for
the children, and social justice programs. Decisions were reached
by voting. After many long hours of meeting and talking, the group
decided to empower girls to be altar servers, an action that did
not take place in the institutional church until 1994. They opted

to use non-canonical scriptural readings. People received communion in their hands prior to the 1973 decree that made this practice permissible.

According to notes on the community provided by long-time member Roberta Brunner, the meetings where these innovations were discussed were "absolutely wild" because of the strong opinions voiced by people finally able to claim their right to speak in church. In spite of the messiness of democracy, leaders of CCS provided a quality liturgy to all attendees each Sunday. The Community of the Christian Spirit has continued to do this for the last thirty-seven years in a variety of iterations and a variety of places.

While a quality, welcoming liturgy was the fundamental mission of the community, for CCS members Sunday liturgy was less an obligation as described in the catechism and more a personal decision to implement the teachings of Jesus into their lives.

Brunner described the glue that held the community together from their inception:

1. Independent thinking and acting
2. A gutsy search for the real meaning of life
3. A madness about all things liturgical
4. An emphasis upon the individual coupled with a passion for consensus
5. A simple longing to worship together happily with song and dance and bread and wine in the Spirit of Jesus.[1]

Brunner and I hope that CCS's challenges, struggles, and growth might serve as an inspiration to those who choose to give birth to a new church community if your bishop declares your present one dead.

INTRODUCTION
DYSTOPIAN MYOPIA

*"There is nothing on this earth so ugly as the
Catholic Church and nothing so beautiful."*

—*Cardinal John Henry Newman*

Popes John Paul II, Benedict XVI, and many in church governance as well as more orthodox believers tend to draw a straight line from Vatican II to the decrease in Mass attendance and the resulting parish closings that are affecting every American diocese. Their rationale for affixing blame varies. Primarily, many critics of the council believe that Vatican II blurred the diametrically opposed concepts of the sacred and the profane. Their hypothesis is that this mix rendered the Mass less sacred and priests less revered. The resulting alleged lack of reverence for the sacred caused secularism to creep in, which in turn displaced faithful religious observance. Secularism made people more selfish, less willing to sacrifice, and, above all, less obedient. As a result, people attended church less frequently. Or so the anti–Vatican II story goes.

The lament for the nineteenth- and early twentieth-century church runs parallel to the criticism of Vatican II: If only the people were as faithful as they were in the good old days! If only more young men would be willing to dedicate their lives to God! Then all manner of things would be well, and the days of the church triumphant would return. The faithful would again pack the churches; the seminaries would fill up again with earnest and dedicated young men; women would again wear their white mantillas to Mass; and Vatican II would look like an anomaly rather than a game changer.

The reality of the last fifty years is, of course, much more complicated. The truth is that everything that ever happens is affected by everything else that is happening. Thus, there are no straight lines or single causes for any particular event but rather a bevy of Venn diagrams whose intersections might be both unwelcome and unpopular but very real. The change in church landscape over the course of the last fifty years did not result directly from the reforms of Vatican II, but rather from the many mass liberation movements that swept the world after World War II of which Vatican II was just one.

These comments are not meant to minimize the effect Vatican II had on the Catholic world. Vatican II took a huge first step in unbinding both the clergy and the laity from a fortress-church straightjacket that had tied them up in liturgical, doctrinal, gender, sacramental, and biblical knots for four hundred years. These knots rendered the liturgy unintelligible, the theology obtuse, the Bible unread, and the gospel message of the Kingdom of God misunderstood. By the late 1950s, the world began moving into a new era. Pope John XXIII realized that the windows of the hierarchical stronghold needed to be opened and new opinions aired because the world had changed and there was no going back to those less than thrilling days of yesteryear that were not really all that awesome for those who did not fit into the institutional narrative of the Roman Catholic Church.

Thus, Vatican II tried to modify the archaic game plan of a church that had become a spectator sport where the pope and the bishops both made the roster and directed every move without consulting the players on the field who oftentimes had better ideas about the direction of the play. The council urged the religious leaders to attend to the signs of the times and to adapt to the demands of their people and listen to them, novel ideas for the time. By the end of the council, the church had adopted reforms that opened the rusty hinges of minds long closed and dedicated to preservation, pomp, and pageantry; permitted worship in the vernacular; gave permission and encouragement to read scripture without a priest's guidance; and, most importantly, empowered the laity.

Historian John O'Malley described the colossal and breathtaking shift in thinking inspired by the council:

> From commands to invitations, from laws to ideals, from definition to mystery, from threats to persuasion, from coercion to conscience, from monologue to dialogue, from ruling to serving, from withdrawn to integrated, from vertical to horizontal, from exclusion to inclusion, from hostility to friendship, from rivalry to partnership, from suspicion to trust... from fault-finding to appreciation, from prescriptive to principled, from behavior modification to *inner* appropriation.[1]

The term "the People of God" grew out of a pastoral heart that wanted to make the church more available, more meaningful, more open and loving to them.

As a person who lived through the changes of Vatican II as a middle schooler, I can recall the enthusiasm I felt as I became an active participant in the revamped Mass, reciting the responses, once reserved for altar boys, first in Latin, and then in English. For the first time, I actually felt as if I was actually worshipping God rather than watching the priest acting in what appeared to be a one-man play with his back towards us, reciting a script in a foreign language that I didn't understand while I followed along in the playbill. For the first time, Sunday Mass was not an obligation. It was actually thrilling to be Catholic as Vatican II began to move Catholics into the modern world.

Sadly, this loving feeling with its accompanying excitement got lost pretty quickly once John Paul II became the pope. John Paul II and his successor, Benedict XVI, restored the old game plan of clerical privilege and mandatory obedience, putting both of their thumbs into the ecclesiastical dike and blocking further reform. At the beginning of the twenty-first century, all these two widely respected religious figures could offer as the way forward in a world suffering from chronic poverty and unending war was a light to a less than stellar past that created the conditions in the first place. The windows of that hopeful, excited pilgrim church with all of its new and promising possibilities were slammed shut and nailed tight. Bishops and far too many priests became John Paul II men—dutiful, obedient, and silent as the Catholic world began to teeter.

In spite of this huge crack in twentieth-first century Roman Catholic life, Pope Emeritus Benedict continued to reiterate his discomfiture with the changes fostered by Vatican II. In a March 2016 interview with *Avvenire*, Benedict stated that the Vatican II created a deep crisis in the church.

What is this deep crisis in the church today? Is it the ongoing economic exploitation of the world's poor? The inability of the world's religions to stop violence and racial hatred? The hypocrisy of a rich church that stands in stark contrast to their founder, who had one robe and no place to lay his head? The sexual abuse scandal and its episcopal cover-up? According to Benedict, the answer, sadly, is none of the above. Instead, Benedict said that the current crisis in the church results from the development of Vatican II ideas that minimize the early fourteenth-century papal doctrine that there is no salvation outside the church.

In his own words, "The missionaries were convinced that the unbaptized person is lost forever. After the [second Vatican] council, this conviction was abandoned. The result was a two-sided deep crisis. Without this attentiveness to salvation, the Faith loses its foundation."[2]

Apparently, the lessons of history seem to have been lost on Benedict. Such one-sided attentiveness to salvation in the great by-and-by—rather than to life on earth as lived by the People of God—often leads people to weep and mourn in a vale of life-long oppression that could easily be stopped by people who are taught by their religious leaders that the cardinal rule of their faith is to love their neighbors as themselves. A fixation upon religious homogeneity and conversion led to the crusades, the massacre of Jews, witch hunts, and the Inquisition, all of which sought to excise the contamination spoiling the purity of the church. It also unleashed the rampant colonialism that reduced native peoples to souls to be saved rather than persons of agency deserving of respect.

The former pontiff seems to have forgotten or ignored the fact that without primary attentiveness to the gospel of love and the Kingdom of God preached by Jesus—accompanied by a modeling of that love—faith strong enough even to move mountains loses its foundation and hypocrisy reigns. It is, instead, the failure to preach gospel values and, most importantly, model and live them that leads to the deep crisis of faith that faces the church today. The secularism and modern reliance upon technology that Benedict castigates has thrown open windows to ecclesiastical sin. As a result, many Catholic people do not like what they see.

It is this chronic disregard for the gospel, the disenchantment with a church that ignored and covered up pedophilia and continues to bully gay people and women, in tandem with the march of historical forces that has led the Roman Catholic Church in America to close Catholic parishes on a grand scale. As a result, former Catholics now constitute the second largest denomination in the United States. In fact, a 2015 Pew survey found that for every one person who joins the Roman Catholic Church, six leave.[3] According to a recent report by the Public Religion Institute in Washington, D.C., Catholicism has the highest rate of attrition of all the major religious denominations.[4]

The scale of parish closures has become unimaginable and will be discussed later in the book. Few American cities have been spared. The Catholic hierarchy, caught between their competing interests in the poor and the need to run and manage a huge institution badly tainted by the sexual abuse scandal that has siphoned off billions of dollars , has claimed that there is simply no other solution to their problem except to close parishes, given the stark reality of statistics. The business model of management indicates that cutting off dead weight allows for a leaner, more streamlined institution. Consequently, the church has learned how to cut its losses, often by starving at-risk parishes of resources and clergy and then declaring them dead.

This behavior is a grave sin, resulting in a smaller presence of the church in many areas, most particularly urban ones. The closings erode the church's ability to spread the good news and harm the most vulnerable of God's people. In closing down parish after parish while refusing to consider alternatives, the Catholic hierarchy has abdicated their responsibility both to God and to the People of God, who increasingly walk away from church once their parish is closed, not because their faith is weak but because the bishops have minimized the importance of local houses of worship and the centrality of the Eucharist in Catholic life. This reality proves the words of Pope Francis: "A church without the Eucharist has no strength."[5]

The bishops have not been held accountable for these mass closures that they claim are inevitable if regrettable. Like the businessmen and -women they hire and emulate, they close parishes for underutilization, which makes perfect sense to everyone but the people sitting in the pews of the parish slated to close. One Philadelphia archdiocesan official exclaimed in complete bafflement to a reporter as a traditional African American parish, founded specifically because black people were once not welcome in white Catholic parishes, was slated to be sold to build million-dollar townhouses for wealthy white people, "I simply don't know how to resolve this issue to their [former parishioners] satisfaction," completely ignoring the devastation and demoralization people feel when their parish is declared dead.[6]

In the face of massive parish closures in the United States, indeed, all over the world, the Roman Catholic Church refuses to consult their own people for alternative solutions and usually disregards those that do. People in Philadelphia, in Boston, and in Cleveland actually offered to either give or raise money for the archdiocese in an effort to keep a specific parish/parishes open. In almost every case, the bishops both refused to meet with the people or consider any alternative to their own plans. Canon law endows the clergy alone with the power of governance. In this model, members of the laity, even those with good ideas and good intentions, remain bit players.

There is another reason for the bishops' behavior. Almost all of the current Roman Catholic bishops were appointed by either John Paul II or Benedict XVI, who equated obedience to the church with obedience to God. These bishops were appointed more for their attention to orthodoxy and less for their pastoral abilities. Just as the two former popes demanded unquestioning obedience from the bishops, so some of these bishops require the same type of obedience from both the faithful and their employees, who must take a loyalty oath that they will adhere to all Catholic doctrine as a criterion for employment. In spite of the current pope's call for mercy, too many of these bishops have persisted in their authoritarian inclinations, supporting or calling for the firing of gay married church employees, investigating theologians, and removing men sympathetic to women's ordination from the priesthood. Several bishops have, in fact, openly criticized the pope for his encyclical *Amoris Laetitia*, which they regard as opening the door for divorced and remarried

Catholics to receive communion. Some John Paul II / Benedict appointees regard Francis as misguided in his attempt to remake the church in the image of the merciful Jesus.[7]

In light of this reality, it is not surprising that rather than listening and learning from the collective experience of their own people, too many members of the Catholic hierarchy continue to proclaim proudly that the church is not a democracy and is thus immune from and unaffected by the opinions and suggestions of their flocks. This top-down, feudal, non-transparent style of government has been discredited by viable governments all over the world. History is littered with the harmful policies of petty dictators and divine-right rulers. The experience of many nations has roundly discredited rule by fiat. Most importantly, the rigid adherence to an archaic form of government that excludes the laity from any type of decision-making short circuits the possibility of transformation and prevents adaptation to the modern world. Closed societies often produce unimaginative solutions to entrenched problems. Unfortunately, it will take a new crop of bishops fashioned in the Francis mode to end this type of governance.

It is time to rethink the organization as well as the thought processes of the institutional Roman Catholic Church. In order to survive in the modern world, the church must be characterized by presence and availability rather than by absence, arbitrary decision making, and, most of all, lack of love and understanding. Desperate times require desperate measures, so experiments in church management, utilization, ministry, mission, liturgy, prayer, and, ultimately, ecclesiology are desperately needed. A diversity of people worships in and belongs to the Catholic Church. That diversity should be reflected in church governance, most particularly in decision-making.

The current reality is that if the official church refuses to travel along a road of imagination and growth, proclaiming the gospel to the ends of the earth, the People of God should consider going alone, hoping that the rest of the church will catch up, as history proves it usually does. This book will offer a blueprint for those with courage to undertake such a journey, a journey pioneered by Jesus himself, who directed all of his followers to preach the good news of the Kingdom of God everywhere and by any means, in spite of religious authorities and regardless of the cost.

Many books such as this offer a disclaimer indicating that those in charge—in this case, the bishops—are really doing their best with the information at their disposal and should not be condemned for engaging in what appears to be a rational plan ensuring survival. The understanding is that good men and women placed in unfortunate circumstances do their best, in good faith, with what they have. However, all human beings, regardless of the factors in their lives or the situations in which they are placed, are accountable for the decisions that they make. They always have a choice.

Thus, the decision to close parishes without lay input or considering other alternatives makes the bishops both complicit and responsible for the current situation.

The reality is that some people, given the same set of circumstances but having a different mindset, might act very differently and formulate very different plans. Including a variety of voices in planning for the future of an enormous number of parishes and an even larger number of Catholics might have produced an entirely different outcome.

Some bishops did and do pretend to consult with the members of their flock. However, many times these consultations were more like an elaborate ruse to manipulate the laity into agreeing with their intention to close parishes.

I was a part of just such a ruse in the late 1990s. The sitting cardinal archbishop of Philadelphia, Anthony Bevilacqua, had been stung by the bad publicity he incurred after a mass closure of inner-city parishes in 1992. While bemoaning the lack of funds necessary to provide an oasis in the desert of poverty for Philadelphia's poorest citizens, Bevilacqua spent considerable funds renovating his New Jersey beach mansion, his grand episcopal residence, and his vesting suite at the cathedral. He disregarded the efforts of a working group of lay Catholics who offered to raise money to keep the inner-city parishes open.

When Bevilacqua decided to close more parishes in the late 1990s, he developed a plan where he clustered parishes into geographical groupings and asked for parish representatives from each parish to meet and chart their own future, allegedly giving power to the people.

The cardinal's plan, however, ensured that poor parishes would be clustered with equally poor parishes, forcing them to share already scarce resources, while the well-to-do were paired with other well-heeled parishes, all of which had considerable resources at their disposal. This plan was very unlike the plans of some Protestant denominations, which had begun partnering poor and wealthy parishes so that the latter could keep the former open. In Bevilacqua's plan, the stronger, wealthier parishes were not even asked if they wanted to support the weaker, poorer parishes.

Instead, in an ecclesiastical version of *The Hunger Games*, the parish representatives from each cluster were instructed to tally up the yearly numbers of baptism and marriages in their respective parishes. These numbers, rather than pastoral care and concern for the poor, determined the survival of each parish. After a couple of meetings, it became clear to me as a working member of the group that the cardinal archbishop had manipulated the lay members of the group into targeting parishes for closure in order to deflect bad press away from him. When I realized that I was expected to affix my name to a document that would close church doors in the faces of my faithful sisters and brothers, I resigned from the group.

Twenty years later, only four of the nine parishes in the cluster that I represented have survived. As a result of this ill-conceived plan, large areas of the sixth largest city in the United States have no functioning Catholic parish.

The seeds for this book were sown during that experience. I worked in the area that suffered the largest number of parish closings in 1992. These areas, largely African American and Latino, had been devastated by the loss of manufacturing jobs when factories moved south or overseas in the 1970s. Poverty, decay, and crime had become the calling cards of a once proud area where jobs were previously plentiful. Schools and recreation centers deteriorated. Houses fell into disrepair. Supermarkets moved out, causing food deserts. Now the Catholic Church was pulling up stakes. It broke my heart to see the church of Jesus abandoning the people who needed them the most.

At the present, no parish, regardless of their bank account or their size, in any diocese can expect to be spared from their bishop's cutting board. If the bishops need money and the number of priests continues to decrease, another round of closures takes place. No parish anywhere is safe.

Those of us who are watching the parish-closing scenario unfold know that there are other ways to adapt to the changing nature of the institutional church in the twenty-first century. The first three chapters of this book highlight the actions of the bishops who fail to realize that they are marching roughshod into a liminal place that requires grace, foresight, and a sense of history, as well as wisdom. The rest of the book is, more importantly, about you, the People of God who are the architects of what will become the future of the church.

One important truth remains in the discussion of the concept of church in the twenty-first century. The church of Jesus Christ should be all about people, about the relationships people form as they worship in a community rather than about money, power, ecclesiastical authority, and enforced obedience. This tenuous bond among community members should be approached with great care, lest it be irreparably damaged and drive people from the Body of Christ. All of the diocesan renewal programs with all of their sounding brass and baseless promises of less being more will fall upon deaf ears unless the beloved community is restored to its pride of place, regardless of where people decide to meet.

May this book give you knowledge, strength, and clarity as you begin your journey into that future where people rather than money and clerical power matter most.

CHAPTER ONE
OPERATION CHAOS

"The suburbanization of the Catholic Church is particularly significant given the longstanding role that Catholic parishes have played in sustaining urban neighborhoods."

—*Anne B. Shlay*

In the 1950s and 1960s, Catholic parishes were bursting at the seams. Catholic baby boomers can remember first-grade classrooms crammed with ninety or more children. Parishes were the hub of activity with Girl and Boy Scouts, the Catholic Youth Organization, dances for teenagers, drama clubs, retreats, missions, novenas, Society of the Sacred Heart, May processions, Forty Hours' Devotion, and Sodalities of the Blessed Mother. These were the halcyon days of Roman Catholicism in America, when community life revolved around the local parish that was manned by a rectory chock-full of priests. Religious sisters graced the front of almost every classroom.

The church of this time was triumphantly filled to the brim with the Church Militant. As the organ thundered and priests dressed in resplendent robes marched down the aisle during Forty Hours' processions preceded by virginal seven-year-old girls dressed in their white Communion dresses who kissed and then threw flower petals on the ground over which the processing men carrying Jesus trod, the faithful knew without a doubt that God was on their side.

By the middle of the 1960s, however, a series of historical forces created a perfect storm that shook this fortress church to its very foundations. In the short space of four decades, these forces transformed traditional Catholic parish life into something entirely different.

As mentioned in the introduction, the spirit of Vatican II began to air out medieval theological concepts that no longer made sense in a modern world. At the same time, mighty liberation movements birthed after World War II washed over the country: civil rights for African Americans, women's rights, and gay rights. The violent, endless, and senseless Vietnam War forced many Americans to rethink America's foreign policies. "My country, right or wrong" and "My church, right or wrong" no longer made any sense to an increasingly educated and vocal populace, as the G.I. Bill provided educational opportunities to large numbers of people who in the past would never have hoped to afford college. Education opened minds. Many Catholics ceased to fear "the pains of hell" and no longer felt obliged to attend weekly Mass or go to confession. College graduates now had as much or more education than their priests and bishops. The priest mystique began to dissipate as the laity saw the clay feet peeping out from under the black cassocks.

Once birth control became readily available in the 1960s, Catholic families, in spite of the fulminations of the church, began to plan their families and thus had fewer children. As the women's liberation movement opened educational doors to professions once dominated by men, fewer women entered the convent or wanted to teach school. Fewer children meant smaller classes, and fewer nuns meant salaries for lay teachers. This caused parish expenses to mount. Parents used to paying for Catholic school via their weekly contributions were now charged tuition that increased every year. Public schools, once feared as a noxious, contaminating influence to be avoided at all costs, became a viable alternative to many Catholic parents who could not afford Catholic school tuition. As a result of this, attendance at Catholic schools plummeted and, with it, church attendance.

Considering all of these factors, it is not surprising that by the early 1980s, the unthinkable began to happen—Catholic churches began to shut their doors.

Unfortunately, the patina of racism covered too many of the early parish closings. In the twentieth century, between twenty and seventy percent of the total population of cities in the Northeast and upper Midwest was Catholic of European descent.[1] By the 1960s, increasing numbers of Catholic people in cities began to move away from their parish of origin and out of the city because they feared African American people, empowered by the civil rights movement, who began moving into previously all-white neighborhoods that had been until then strictly segregated. According to historian John McGreevy, more Irish Catholics fled from American cities in the twentieth century than left Ireland in any decade of the nineteenth century.[2]

The out-migration of huge numbers of Catholics from the city to the suburbs reconfigured the cities, along with the surrounding areas, as diocesan officials followed the people with the money to the suburbs, building spanking-new, well-appointed parishes, often right outside the city limits to accommodate them. This explosive growth plastered hundreds of thousands of acres once devoted to farming and parkland with cookie-cutter housing developments and strip malls, set amidst these brand-new Catholic parishes and schools.

The suburban population in the Philadelphia area, for instance, increased by one hundred percent in the last third of the twentieth century. By 2000 there were more Catholics in the suburbs than there were in the city. As a result, the Archdiocese of Philadelphia took on a distinctly suburban flair, upgrading itself into a largely homogeneous white suburban church. The inner-city parishes went into a steep decline from which they would not recover.[3]

White flight caused perfectly functioning, architecturally beautiful parishes in the city to deteriorate as congregations shrank and parishes lost income. As a result, these lovely, once vibrant buildings degraded into what New York's Archbishop Timothy Dolan has labeled "the suffocating museums," which he is closing all over New York City.

Most Blessed Sacrament parish (MBS), located in a lovely residential section of west Philadelphia, is a poster child for urban church decline that resulted directly from white flight. Founded in 1901, it once boasted the largest Catholic elementary school in the entire world. White flight through the 1970s and 1980s decimated the parish, and by the late 1980s, MBS fell on hard times. Its death knell sounded in 1999 when it was twinned with another parish. By 2007, the parish was officially declared dead and stripped of its art work and relics.

Urban parish closures across the country followed the same pattern as Most Blessed Sacrament. First, as mentioned previously, parishes in racially isolated areas, poor areas, and working-class areas were closed first as white people moved out, causing a decrease in Mass attendance that translated into smaller collections. The various dioceses then allowed inner-city parishes to die a slow death as needed repairs became too expensive to fix from the contents of diminished collection baskets. It finally became cheaper and, according to the church, financially wiser to close them, harvesting statues and art works for resale or reassignment to suburban parishes that were remodeled with treasures paid for by the dead parish's former members. This process left vast swaths of the inner cities studded with rotting church hulks.

Patrick Hildebrandt describes the wholesale abandonment process on his blog *Philadelphia Church Project*:

> Remember, this is a group [the Archdiocese of Philadelphia] whose past behavior includes ignoring sanctuaries until their roofs are collapsing, closing healthy parishes in hot residential areas and trying to sell their bones for a profit, taking hatchets to building interiors without regard for their inherent artistry, and steamrolling over the wishes and desires of the faithful.[4]

The church never seemed to understand the consequences of their actions as they closed parishes in the faces of the urban poor while simultaneously opening new ones for the well-to-do in the suburbs. It is people's choice to live where they want to live, as the late Cardinal Bevilacqua explained to a Philadelphia community activist in 2002. He, the cardinal archbishop of a great city who felt empowered to instruct people on the intimate details of their sex lives, could not tell them not to run away from their sisters and brothers of color. Nowhere in his belated 1998 pastoral letter entitled "Healing Racism through Faith and Truth" did Bevilacqua address the church's role in supporting white flight.[5]

By the early years of the twenty-first century, *choice* had become a buzzword shared by people and clergy alike to cover up the racism that continued to persist in spite of a widespread and largely shared belief that Americans now lived in a color-blind society. Choice coupled with taste, rather than overt prejudice of generations past, came to determine Catholics' place of residence and where they sent their children to school. With this belief firmly attached to their psyche, bishops like Anthony Bevilacqua and their flocks easily absolved themselves of any hint that they might be just as racist as their forbearers, who often resorted to violence to enforce neighborhood segregation.

The blinders provided by this much-touted color blindness prevented church leaders from seeing the poorest and most vulnerable members of their flocks. When the Philadelphia Archdiocese planned a synod in 2002 that was supposed to set the tone for Catholicism in the new century, all of the planning meetings were scheduled to take place in the suburbs, where most white Catholics now lived, far away from their sisters and brothers of color. Consequently, little in the synod agenda concerned racism and ongoing white flight.

When a few people complained, the archdiocese grudgingly held just one planning session within the city limits. Unfortunately, the synod attendees and decision makers chose not to address racism in any coherent fashion. I attended the only break-out session dedicated specifically to racism. Three other elderly white people attended. The bulk of the meeting consisted in praying that racism would end.

Two members of the synod's Topical Commission on Moral and Social Issues, which included racism, resigned their position because the cardinal ignored their recommendations and the final draft of the synod failed to include any coherent reference to racism.[6]

Parishes in wealthier and more stable areas of the cities and the suburbs—most of whom stood by silently as parish after parish was closed in the faces of their sisters and brothers of color in poorer areas—believed that their wealth and prestige provided them with immunity from the diocesan hatchet. By the early years of the twenty-first century, the unthinkable began to happen. Wealthy parishes, many of which sat upon desirable acreage, learned to their chagrin that their solvent, well-attended parishes were being targeted for closure as the priest and dollar shortage became more acute.

At the present, no parish anywhere is safe from the diocesan "renewal" plans designed by local bishops. As Betsy Bohlen, the chief operating officer of the Archdiocese of Chicago, obfuscated while discussing upcoming parish closings and mergers, "Even very vibrant parishes in affluent communities are less effective than they could be if they collaborated."[7] In other words, your debt-free parish with its filled-to-capacity Masses, bible study, and scout troops could be next on the chopping block.

In 2014, Mark Gray of the Center for Applied Research in the Apostolate (CARA) recorded the startling fact that nine percent of all parishes in the United States have closed since 2000. This figure translates into 1,753 fewer parishes nationwide.[8] The beat continues to go on and on each year with increasing numbers of parishes closing and merging nationwide.

In the five-county Archdiocese of Philadelphia, for instance, the number of parishes has been reduced from 279 to 219 with the Archdiocese indicating that there are more closures to follow. Many of these parishes had money in the bank and high weekly attendance at Mass.[9]

Philadelphia is not alone in suffering non-transparent parish closings and unreceptive bishops. In New York City, where the archdiocesan reorganizational plan is euphemistically branded "Making All Things New," Wall Street Archbishop Timothy Dolan intends to merge 112 parishes to create 55 new parishes. Thirty-one parishes will close.[10] In racially diverse East Harlem, three out of seven parishes will shut their doors.[11]

Chicago, too, seeks to unload its inner city parishes and restructure the entire archdiocese in its rosily titled plan "Renew My Church." According to the archdiocesan plan, one hundred parishes will close in the next fourteen years.[12]

In 2004, Boston decided to close one out of every five parishes. Prior to the Boston Globe's exposure of priest pedophilia and its cover-up, there were 357 parishes in Boston.[13] Eighty-two have been closed.[14]

In Saginaw, Michigan, the bishop reduced the number of parishes in mid-Michigan from 109 to 53.[15]

In 2008, almost half of the parishes in the Camden, New Jersey, diocese, which contains one of the poorest cities in the nation, closed,[16] as did 91 out of 209 parishes in Scranton, Pennsylvania and 47 of 151 parishes in its neighboring city, Allentown.[17]

There is only one remaining Catholic parish in the entire city of Chester, Pennsylvania, one of the poorest cities in Pennsylvania.[18]

The number of parishes in Sioux City, Iowa, decreased from 108 to just 67.[19]

In Cleveland, 29 out of 224 parishes have closed and 41 have consolidated.[20]

Mergers or twinning or clustering of parishes are usually a death warrant that destabilizes all of the parishes that are tossed together in a diocesan dice roll. Hildebrandt calls the twinning process, "Dead Twin Walking." Who survives and who closes? Only the diocese knows for sure. There is another, sneaky side to the merger story. Since the treasuries of the parishes remain separate from that of the dioceses, the working parish in the relationship, rather than the diocese, is forced to shoulder the weaker parish's debt, as well as the maintenance and repair of the physical plant. It doesn't take long for the parish with the full-time pastor to realize that he needs to shed his weaker twin in order to survive. In the dog-eat-dog diocesan financial world, only the strong parish will remain open for Mass on Sunday morning.

Merging parishes creates other types of problems. When parishes are vacated and the "For Sale" sign appears on the front door, the parishioners know that their parish is truly dead. However, the parish into which they are merged is also declared dead by the diocese, a fact that the members of the surviving parish that maintains its name and worship site often do not understand. With the merger, the diocese forms a new corporation that absorbs both the existing and the dead parishes. The resulting entity is officially a new and different parish even as the name of the parish remains the same.

Parishioners who do not realize that the diocese has killed off their parish with the merger and established a new and different one often believe that they have become a host church for their neighbors, who are often regarded as long-term guests. The welcome wagon loses some of its traction when it seems as if the merged members are "taking over" their parish when it is, in fact, no longer their parish or even the same parish.

In one particular case, white members of a vibrant, integrated parish were regarded by some as racists when they objected to some changes in the liturgy that were made without any input or explanation. However, no one had informed them that when they absorbed two largely African American parishes that their own parish had died and that the new parish needed to become something new and different if all were to survive. Hard feelings drove some people away from a church that had been a model for diversity in a largely non-diverse archdiocese.

Priests in Cologne, Germany, aptly expressed the dissatisfaction felt by both priests and their congregations as church leaders merge parishes. Calling clustering an "imposition," the priests said that closing and merging parishes "furthers the anonymization and isolation that is already taking place in society." Parish priests, they wrote, should be available to people in their local parish, in the sight of their familiar spire.[21]

While parishioners mourn the end of their parish life as they knew it, the bishops cast blame and seem to draw a blank as they crunch the numbers. The exponential growth of Pentecostal and non-denominational churches in areas once served by Catholic parishes prove that people are hungry for God. Thus, Catholic bishops have not taken advantage of that spiritual hunger by finding creative ways to keep parishes open. In relying on an outmoded membership model of church where Sunday head counts and collection tallies determine parish survival, the bishops have forgotten the communities that God has bequeathed to them for safe keeping. Rather than examining their own consciences, bishops like Thomas Tobin of Providence, Rhode Island, attribute the decrease in Mass attendance to their flock's lack of faith, rather than to their

own, thus absolving themselves of any hint of blame for the ongoing crisis.

> If your faith is strong, you go to church because you know it
> fulfills a divine command. There's a tendency nowadays to
> overlook the concept of "obligation" in things both religious
> and secular. An entitled generation thinks that when they at-
> tend Mass, they're doing God a favor, when, in fact, they have a
> sacred obligation to do so and that it's offensive to God if they
> deliberately ignore him![22]

Charles Zech, director of the Center for Church Management
and Business Ethics at Villanova University outside of Philadelphia,
said that the parish closings would have been easier if the situation
had been handled earlier. One might ask, which situation might that
have been? The situation where the bishops failed to address the
mass movement of white Catholics to the suburbs away from their
African American sisters and brothers that began in the 1960s and
continued into the 1990s? Their tacit support of that flight as they
continued to buy up land and build new churches in the suburbs?

Plans to maintain existing churches were, indeed, developed but
not by the Catholic Church. In spite of the bishops writing collective and individual pastoral letters condemning racism, other faiths
engaged in local, practical activities that paved the way to peaceful integration.

In 1959, for example, a Philadelphia rabbi named Elias Charry
visited every single member of his congregation, Germantown Jewish Centre, when it became clear that the neighborhood was euphemistically going to "change," urging them not to move away from
their sisters and brothers of color. While he and his congregation
planned for the then unknowns of living and worshipping in an
integrated neighborhood, too many Catholic priests remained silent while their white parishioners fled to the suburbs. As a result

of Charry's efforts, the neighborhood surrounding the synagogue provided a model for peaceful urban integration.

Thirty-three years later, as more and more Philadelphia neighborhoods slipped into poverty, Cardinal Bevilacqua prohibited priests from remaining in a group called Philadelphia Interfaith Action (PIA), an ecumenical organization composed of Catholic, African American, and Protestant clergy who had worked together for four years in an effort to prevent community disintegration that would lead to parish closings. He issued his ban one week before an opening assembly that was scheduled to take place in February of 1992. The news was so upsetting than an African American clergyman who had worked closely with the Catholic clergy on this project cried when he heard the news. All of the priests withdrew obediently, and the process of neighborhood disintegration continued.[23] The following year the cardinal closed thirteen parishes and seven schools in the very area PIA was trying to save.

Minus a good example from the cardinal archbishop of Philadelphia and the widespread preaching of a gospel of love, white Catholics left their neighborhoods—and their parishes—en masse. A Catholic parish located in a community adjoining Germantown Jewish Centre transitioned from being ninety-eight percent Caucasian to ninety-eight percent African American in a mere two years.[24] On the other hand, Germantown Jewish Centre, a shining synagogue upon a hill, remains large and vibrant, while nearby Catholic parishes have been closed or twinned. As this book goes to press, two additional parishes in this area are in the process of being sold.

Rather than visiting their parishioners and urging them not to flee their sisters and brothers of color, the bishops advocated evangelization techniques to bump up church attendance in flagging areas that sometimes bordered on the ridiculous. During a time of mass closures in 2005, the evangelization method offered on the Philadelphia archdiocesan website was to advise parishioners to tell their non-Catholic neighbors to visit the local priest. Aside from touting the September 2015 visit of the pope and the World Meeting of Families, the same website suggested that parishioners engage their pastors in a game called "Stump Your Priest" to drum up interest.

Or could the situation for which the church needed to have planned been the sharp decrease in the number of celibate, male Catholic priests, a model that the Church has continued to support in spite of its ongoing failure? Whether the situation was white flight or a burgeoning priest shortage, both of these issues were clearly evident to those who had eyes to see thirty years ago.

On the face of it, closing parishes with low attendance and little financial support seems inevitable. Many Protestant churches began their outward movement to the suburbs in the 1950s, as did most synagogues. At the present, some Protestant denominations have tried to maintain their presence in poor neighborhoods by enlisting the support and finances of wealthy communities.

Few would dispute the idea that good business practices should dictate the utilization of scarce resources. The problem lies, however, with the high-handed and non-transparent manner in which the closings in the Catholic archdioceses are being done.

While New York's Timothy Dolan expressed the frustration of bishops when he said they are "being strangled by trying to maintain the behemoth of institutional Catholicism," he did not follow canon law when he announced massive parish closings in 2015, a move that included well-attended parishes with no debt that didn't fit this definition of decline.[25] According to canon law, the bishop must follow two steps when closing a parish: first, announce the closing; second, state his rationale for closing it. Instead, Dolan merely had pastors announce closings to stunned parishioners at Mass and then refused to explain his rationale to the people afterward. When challenged on his failure to follow protocol, a diocesan spokesperson called Dolan's failure to act appropriately "an oversight." The canon lawyer representing eight of the parishes slated for closure called Dolan's misconceived closures "chaos."[26]

Dolan, like Tobin, remains oblivious to the harm he has caused his flock. In a letter to the clergy written in November, 2016, Dolan wrote that the most pressing problem in his archdiocese is "a mistrust of, and antagonism towards the archdiocese." He also criticized Catholics for not tithing like other faiths. Missing from the letter was any sort of self-reflection on why people without a voice either in their local parishes or in the church at large might not want to contribute to a church that does not regard them as equal partners.[27]

In the very next issue of the *National Catholic Reporter*, Susan Coleman, a member of Dolan's flock responded in a letter to the editor.

Thank you so much for your article about Cardinal Timothy Dolan's letter urging parish leaders to be less timid and more aggressive in their attempts to extract cash from their parishioners.

I found the tone of the letter to be very bold and the content shamefully naïve. I think most people enjoy giving money to their favorite charities or houses of worship. We give because we want to support their work and show our approval for their efforts. We give to causes and organizations that we believe in, that we trust, admire, and take pride in.

Dolan and many of the people working in the offices of the New York archdiocese do absolutely nothing to make us want to give to the church. Their actions, decrees, and words are final—not open to reasonable discussion or recourse, with no regard for the feelings of scores of generous, devout Catholics. Their behavior is shameful for its lack of honesty, transparency, and compassion.

A case in point would be the closure of Our Lady of Peace Church in New York City. Any reasonable person familiar with the "facts" regarding the closure of this one little church and the extraordinary measures its parishioners have gone to get the church reopened—and the way they have been treated by Dolan and the archdiocese—is enough to ignite a sense of shame and shock. Why, in heaven's name, would I want to support church with leaders like this? I certainly don't and obviously neither do many others.[28]

The *New York Daily News* reported that the Archdiocese of New York—while claiming that it was all an accident—sent locksmiths to change the locks on the doors of Our Lady of Peace while the shocked and insulted people were inside attending their last Mass together as a parish.[29]

The other issue is that Jesus did not intend the church to be a business. In fact, the goals of those who follow gospel values should be very different from the goals of business people who adhere to the bottom line. The catechism of the Catholic Church is quite clear about the role of business in the life of human beings:

> The development of economic activity and growth in production are meant to provide for the needs of the human being. Economic life is not meant solely to multiply goods and increase profits and power; it is ordered first to the service of human beings. Economic activity, conducted according to its own proper methods, is to be exercised within the limits of the moral order, in keeping with social justice so as to correspond to God's plan for humanity.[30]

Should the church of Jesus Christ be run like a business? Can a church be both and survive? Jesus was quite clear about the route his followers were supposed to take:

> No one can serve two masters. Either you will hate the one and love the other, or you will be devoted to the one and despise the other. You cannot serve both God and money.[31]

Unfortunately, a church run like a business de-centers Christ and replaces him and the gospel of love with good business practices designed by the demands of an impersonal market whose goal is to make money for its stockholders.

That market now sets the tone for every aspect of American life, apparently even faith life. The market that has displaced Jesus from the very heart of the Catholic Church requires a corporate life complete with company accoutrements, including diocesan PR representatives who wax eloquent as they try to explain how less is really more and how the people really will benefit when they have to walk or drive longer distances to church. In fact, the PR people for many of the dioceses dress up the parish closings in flowery language to disguise the fact that the pearl of great price that they are hawking is really a fake from the dollar store. Like the corporations they mimic, Catholic dioceses made little effort to explore the effects the closing of a large Catholic parish has on the surrounding neighborhood, most particularly in poorer areas that are already lacking in amenities like supermarkets and public schools. Instead, they couch business deals in theological language in an effort to make their business plans more palatable.

Kenneth Gavin, the spokesman for the Archdiocese of Philadelphia, in 2015 described the huge Catholic absence in many areas of the city as a means to create "vibrant" and "sustainable" parishes—obviously in some other neighborhood. While the archdiocese claims to be aware of people's pain, Gavin advised the people that these drastic diminishments were necessary to "ensure a strong church for the future."[32]

The Archdiocese of Philadelphia is not alone. Cardinal Cupich dressed up the planned massive closures in Chicago by stating, "By having the boldness to leave behind familiar ways of doing things, we can seize this season as one that is not simply of loss, but rather of renewal."[33] One of the familiar ways of doing things that could be left behind might be individual wedding ceremonies. According to one Chicago pastor, couples in the future should expect that they will have to share their wedding day with other wedding couples because of the ongoing priest shortage.[34]

Bishop David Zubik of Pittsburgh, Pennsylvania, labeled the downsizing of his diocese "On Mission for the Church Alive!" as he planned for the immediate closure of fifteen struggling parishes.[35]

The city of Rochester, New York, is already feeling this new way of doing church. A priest told a woman whose mother was dying that he, as pastor of several parishes, could not promise that he could preside at her mother's funeral. A family in Philadelphia was directed to find their own priest if they wished to have their funeral in the parish where the deceased was baptized. Priests can provide Mass at nursing homes located in their parishes several times a year, if that. Increasing numbers of priests across the nation feel constrained not to provide graveside ceremonies after funerals because there are no other priests in their area to provide emergency pastoral care. A suburban parish outside of Philadelphia outfitted an aged and physically compromised priest with a special throne-like chair so that he could continue to preside at Mass because there was no one to take his place.

One must wonder what type of renewed church the hierarchy is really planning for in the near future. Can the good news be preached far and wide by drastically shrinking the number of pulpits and curtailing the celebration of the Eucharist? Most importantly, what happens when survival mode trumps mission? In curtailing its sense of mission and focusing solely upon survival, the Catholic Church ultimately ignores the wants and needs of the People of God and serves as a mortician overseeing the death of hundreds of parishes rather than as a midwife birthing something new.

The sad reality is that closing down churches and making the Eucharist—the summit of Catholic worship—into a scarce commodity ensures that the church will eventually become irrelevant to the People of God as worship becomes something one might do on Sunday if one does not have other pressing things to do. If the church does not find the Eucharist to be important enough to provide it every week to the People of God, why should the People of God bother coming to church? If the church leadership does not choose to sacrifice its assets in order to preserve the mission given to it by Jesus to demonstrate the love of God to the world, why should anyone else bother to sacrifice anything?

Business executives use numbers as their plumb line. It should not be the way the church works, especially a church that expects its own people to make considerable and heroic sacrifices in their own lives, most especially a church that claims to exist outside of and above the secular world.

There is a view from the pews that the bishops ignore at their own peril. To continue to shutter parishes in the face of parishioner protests and call it renewal is both foolish and ill-advised. The People of God have come of age and will no longer bow to ecclesiastical imperatives without a fight. Or, they will thumb their noses at their bishop and simply walk away from a church that sustained their ancestors for generations. Tens of thousands have already taken this path.

Although He promised us he would be with us until the end of time, Jesus didn't guarantee that the current parish structure manned by celibate, male priests would last unto the generations. By His resurrection, Jesus taught us that He can transform and enliven everything, even the parishes that your bishop has declared dead. Those planning for the future must have the faith and the vision and the heart that the bishops lack.

The following chapters of this book will discuss the ways that you, a faithful parishioner, can keep your parish alive and well in a new and different way. As always, the Holy Spirit will point the way. Jesus always knocks at our door. It is up to the People of God to let Him enter.

Chapter Two
The Magic Christians

"Behind every great fortune, there lies great crime."

—*Honoré de Balzac*

In chapter one I mentioned some societal causes for the decrease in Mass attendance: universal education, women's liberation, civil rights, birth control, and hierarchical intransigence in the face of change. Each of these things could merit a book of its own.

For our purposes, I'd like to elaborate upon two issues that fall under the category of hierarchical intransigence: the church's ongoing lack of accountability for the money that is collected and the chronic lack of celibate, male priests. While the church cannot control history and mass movements, it can, if it chooses, manage its finances and personnel.

Two huge questions arise from these two issues. How can the church not have enough money to keep parishes open when its estimated wealth hovers between nine and ten billion euros, when it has enough money for matching fancy vestments at special events, palatial homes for bishops and cardinals, hundreds of thousands of dollars in lobbyist fees, and frequent junkets to Rome?

Secondly, why would that same church continue to rely upon a male celibate model of priesthood which has proven to be unsustainable for the last two generations?

Let's begin with the money.

In spite of the seemingly empty coffers of American dioceses which have been forced by a lack of funds to close almost two thousand parishes across the nation, the American church contributes an astounding amount of money to support the Vatican and its enterprises even though the Vatican is apparently awash in billions of euros of its own. One must wonder why the cash flow is not going the other way.

Merchants in the Temple by Gianluigi Nuzzi and *Avarizia* (avarice) by Emiliano Fittipaldi highlight the huge amounts of money gathering interest—and dust—in the accounts of various Vatican departments:

- The Commission of Cardinals—425,000 euros
- Account for Holy Masses—2.7 million euros
- Peter's Pence 2013—378 million euros[1]

Foundations named for late popes sit untouched in accounts totaling more than 15 million euros. Nuzzi described Vatican finances as "an incredible waste of money by the men who govern the church."[2]

Vatican City, the smallest nation on earth, has the most complex bureaucracy in the world with fourteen human resources departments staffed by people with vague job descriptions who earn large amounts of money doing their own thing. Money runs literally runs through their fingers. According to Nuzzi, few of these employees could even provide a yearly report to regulators of what he described as the "massive circulation of money inside the Vatican." Instead, the Vatican is characterized by a "complete absence of transparency in bookkeeping."[3]

For instance, two years ago, Vatican finance minister Cardinal George Pell reported that he had found an additional 1.5 billion euros stashed away in various departmental accounts. The finding of a vast amount of money hidden away as pin money in a couple of drawers was casually dismissed by Carlo Marroni, a reporter for Italy's leading financial newspaper: "Its [the Vatican's] balance sheets are worth billions of euros, so the findings are not even particularly crucial to their budget."[4]

Rome is not alone in finding hidden money. On February 18, 2015, the Associated Press revealed that the diocese of Cologne, Germany, sits upon a fortune of 3.8 billion euros.[5]

Very little of this enormous amount of money is donated to charity because charity, apparently, begins at home, in the Vatican. In January, 2016, the *Catholic Herald* reported that only two out of every ten euros collected for Peter's Pence, a charitable collection to fund occasions that the pope decides are emergencies, are actually used for charity. The remainder of Peter's Pence is used for the upkeep of the Roman Curia.[6]

Pope Francis has tried to breach the Teflon coat that seems to protect holy money from sinful men by instituting controls at the much-maligned Vatican bank, once the source of uncontrolled money laundering. Philip Willan wrote in *The Guardian* that prior to Francis, the money at the Vatican bank was managed with "promiscuous generosity," with bank administrators taking money paid by the faithful, who expected Masses for their dead, and donating it to friends and pet causes. In 1984, the bank paid out the enormous sum of 240 million euros to creditors to make up for banking irregularities that took place throughout the 1970s.[7] This money had been donated in good faith by the People of God for charitable purposes.

Even as Francis tried to clean up the bank, the "promiscuous generosity" persisted in other Vatican departments. In 2013, Nunzio Scarano, the top accountant in charge of Vatican investments and real estate, was able to accumulate a fortune estimated at 8.2 million euros while earning a humble salary of $41,000 euros. Scarano lived in a 7,500-square-foot, 17-room luxury apartment whose walls were covered with 6 million euros worth of art. "Donations" from satisfied parishioners, he said, endowed his luxurious lifestyle.[8]

Fittipaldi also reported that raiding charities to pay for nice digs is not all that unusual in Vatican City. He reported that nearly half a million euros were diverted from a foundation that funded a children's hospital in Rome to cover the costs of renovating the splendidly appointed rooftop palace of Cardinal Tarcisio Bertone, the former Vatican secretary of state. Bertone employs three nuns to cook for him in a kitchen worthy of first place in a "House Beautiful" magazine, polish the 2,400 square feet of an oak parquet floor, and answer the doorbell attached to a 6,000 euro front security door.

After coming under fire for living like the prince he believes himself to be, Bertone pouted, "Scores of other prelates live in even nicer apartments," many rent free as the Vatican department overseeing real estate is owed 4 million euros in unpaid rent.[9]

Bertone is absolutely correct in his assessment of "nice" apartments, even for those who no longer work at the Vatican. The former head of the Prefecture for the Economic Affairs of the Holy See lives with two nuns in a 4,780-square-foot apartment. He had the gall to comment that his apartment was "nothing luxurious."

When asked why members of the Curia don't move from their large, lavish apartments to rooming houses like Pope Francis to save money, Archbishop Angelo Becciu, a top official in the Vatican Secretariat of State replied that such a question is "populist bordering on the ridiculous."[10]

This style of living persists in spite of the example of simple living Pope Francis tries to project by living in a guesthouse. In spite of the papal exhortation that bishops and cardinals should be like "shepherds with the smell of sheep," his minions continue to pursue the luxurious lifestyles of the 1%.

The Catholic Church in the United States accounts for approximately 60% of the church's global wealth. Because of this great wealth, the American church provides almost all of the funding that is needed to renovate and restore buildings in Rome.[11] Thus, the words of New York's Cardinal Timothy Dolan—that he and other American cardinals are being "strangled by trying to maintain the behemoths of institutional Catholicism" from the early twentieth century—ring hollow when there is no problem, apparently, in sending astronomical amounts of money to Europe to maintain and remodel the magnificent palaces Catholicism inherited from the sixteenth century.

The members of the Roman Curia are, of course, not alone in pursuing sumptuous lifestyles. Opulence comes with the episcopal territory. In 1998, journalist Ralph Cipriano described the lavish spending habits of former Philadelphia Cardinal Anthony Bevilacqua, who spent enormous amounts of money refurbishing his mansion and shore house, as well as expensive accoutrements for the archdiocesan offices and cathedral, while simultaneously shutting down largely black and Hispanic parishes in Philadelphia's vulnerable inner city.[12]

Bevilacqua is not alone. Jason Berry, a frequent chronicler of ecclesiastical faux pas, described former Archbishop Anthony Pilla of Cleveland as "living like a lord" in a house with six bedrooms, a pond, and tennis courts.[13]

In 2014, CNN's Daniel Burke wrote about the wealthy lifestyles of bishops who live in tastefully appointed homes that are sometimes worth millions of dollars. Burke reported that Dolan's New York City mansion on Madison Avenue is worth thirty million dollars. Bishops John Myers of Newark and Thomas Wenski of Miami have swimming pools, and Wenski has a tiki bar.[14] Like their confrere Anthony Bevilacqua, some bishops were spending hundreds of thousands of dollars on their homes while simultaneously closing parishes and ending important programs for the poor due to an alleged lack of funds.

In a March 2016 article, *The Huffington Post* described the plush lodgings that are made available to American bishops visiting Rome. The impeccably appointed Villa Stritch, recently renovated to the tune of $715,000, includes a bar with five taps costing $10,000 and light switches that cost $2,000. The fireplace cost $30,000 and the specially treated Sicilian marble floor $30,000, with an extra $18,000 thrown in to project a more brilliant shine. The decorator spent $300,000 to renovate a small reception room. This Roman home away from home for American Catholic bishops is maintained by a restricted fund of $18,000,000.[15]

To top off the majesty and pomp provided for men for whom money is no obstacle, priests and bishops appear in resplendently lavish identical vestments during local events or in Rome. During the pope's visit to the United States in September of 2015, hundreds of bishops and priests appeared multiple times in different, magnificently matching vestments. One comedian joked that the Vatican purchases more lace than Victoria's Secret. When a bishop is named by the pope, the first thing he does is fly to Rome and purchase the appropriate episcopal uniform, a watered silk cassock and red cummerbund. Cardinals such as Raymond Burke pay more for their vestments than a starlet does for the dress she wears to the Academy Awards.

Too much unaccountable money creates another set of problems for those who consider themselves redeemed. In March 2017, *The National Catholic Reporter* documented a Vatican City court's investigation of possible financial crime, including money laundering at the Vatican bank that led to the freezing of $2.1 million dollars. This amount adds to the already vast sum of $11.3 million dollars already frozen due to banking irregularities at the Vatican bank from 2012 through 2016, where twenty-three irregular transactions were noted.[16]

The idea that spending loose, fast, and generally unaccountable money is permissible under divine guidance often trickles down to the parish level. A former head of a parish council described the ecclesiastical mentality: that God will always somehow provide the money the church needs to run itself. Consequently, money is no object for the men who owe their livelihood to the church.

In addition, according to church security expert Michael W. Ryan, "tens of millions" of dollars are embezzled from collection baskets across the United States *annually* both by pastors and parishioners. Ryan wrote that the United States Conference of Catholic Bishops' (USCCB) refusal under canon law 455 to impose uniform guidelines on safeguarding the Sunday collection in every American diocese leads to the embezzlement of this vast sum of money by both pastors and those who have been chosen to count money donated by the faithful.[17]

According to Berry, and confirmed by the 2015 books of Nuzzi and Fittipaldi, far too much of the money donated by the laity to the church is misdirected, untraceable, unaccounted for, placed in slush funds, laundered, paid out in making reparations for the mismanagement of the child abuse scandal, or just plain lost. Although many American dioceses do now publicly post their financial statements each year, accounts managed by Rome and by most dioceses remain largely opaque and, according to canon lawyer Sister Kate Kuenstler, who has represented many parishes targeted for closure, flush with easy and readily available cash. While individual parishes might film the counting of the collection basket, that basket often remains open and unsecured from the time it leaves the sanctuary until it reaches the counting room.

Because of this fast and loose system of handling money, Archbishop Rembert Weakland of Milwaukee was able to buy off a former male lover with $450,000 belonging to his diocese.[18]

Former New York Cardinal Edward Egan serves as the bishops' poster boy for financial opacity. When asked by a *New York Times* reporter if he would open his books to the public for scrutiny, Egan replied, "Do we want to leave ourselves open? Oh, what fun people could have!"[19]

The sexual abuse scandal in the United States has created another unholy financial mess. In the November 2015 issue of the *National Catholic Reporter*, Jack Ruhl and Diane Ruhl reported that the U.S. Catholic Church spent nearly 4 billion dollars as a result of the sexual abuse scandal. This did not include the amount spent by bishops on lobbying efforts to fight extending the statute of limitations.[20]

In spite of multiple, mind-numbing grand jury reports from cities across the country that have documented the cover-up of sexual abuse by multiple bishops, too many of them continue to wound survivors and their families by fighting statutes of limitations. *The Economist* estimated that Cardinal Timothy Dolan spent between a hundred thousand and a million dollars on fighting statutes of limitations in New York.[21] The Archdiocese of Philadelphia announced in their 2016 Catholic Charities Appeal that some of the charitable donations collected during that appeal would be diverted to the Pennsylvania Catholic Conference, a lobby that fights the extension of these statutes. In early 2017, the New York Times reported that Cardinal Dolan hopes to take out a $100 million mortgage to compensate victims who have filed sexual abuse claims against the Archdiocese of New York.[22]

How did a church that purports to follow its founder—Jesus Christ, who had one robe and no place to lay his head—come to accumulate such wealth? How can bishops who vacation in Villa Stritch and warm themselves before a fireplace costing 30,000 euros turn the poor out of their parish home? The money that drops like gentle rain from heaven in Rome and in the palatial homes of the bishops is curiously absent at the parish level. There the tithing is measured and found wanting as the weightier parts of Jesus' message are oddly ignored.

The laity that supplies the bishops with their salaries, their mansions, and their junkets to Rome, as well as the upkeep of the Vatican, is entitled to know how their hard-earned money is spent. Most importantly, men in an institution sitting upon billions of dollars in assets should not be crying poor and shutting the doors of the churches in the faces of the faithful.

However, the elephant in that tastefully decorated episcopal living room that tramps right through the thicket of pious publicity surrounding parish closures is, of course, the rapidly diminishing number of priests. The declining number of priests worldwide is staggering. In the United States alone, the number of priests declined from 58,632 in 1975 to 38,275 in 2014, a reduction of 33 percent. There are few replacements for those who leave, retire, or die since the number of seminarians has dropped by an astounding 85 percent.[23]

A 2015 article in *The Irish* Times exemplifies hierarchical wooden-headedness in the face of a worsening priest shortage. Papal Nuncio to Ireland Charles Brown told reporter Patsy McGarry that in Ireland there is a huge "crisis in numbers... [that] will, in the short term, not get better." Brown claimed that it is only in 2015 that Ireland is beginning to feel the pinch of the vocational shortage as priests in their 70s and 80s die off with very few replacements in the offing.[24] Ireland is not the only country in this predicament.

Brown's comments are perplexing in light of the documented decrease in the number of priests over the last three decades. It is only in 2015 that Ireland is feeling the dearth of priests? Has the rapidly diminishing number of priests escaped the bishops as they refuse to consider the necessary steps they need to take in order to stave off the catastrophic priest shortage—not only in Ireland, but also in the rest of the Western world—even as the lack of priests reported in individual dioceses has been both ongoing and breathtaking for two generations? As one parish after another falls victim to the priest shortage, the clarion call of the pope and the bishops is for more vocations of the male celibate type, the type that has been disappearing for the last forty years.

According to CARA, there are now 3,499 parishes without a resident priest, up from 2,843 in 2000, a net increase of 23 percent. The number of active priests per parish has also decreased from 1.2 to 1. For every 100 priests who die or leave ministry, there are only 30 to 40 to replace them.[25]

The statistics provided by Future Church listed below are breath-taking.

After closing 40 of its 170 parishes in 2010, the Diocese of Syracuse had only 100 priests left to serve the remaining 130 parishes. Forty of those priests were age 75 or older. Other dioceses follow the same alarming trend. Future Church estimates that by 2027, there will be only 76 active priests in Cleveland serving 820,000 Catholics.[26]

The Diocese of Altoona/Johnstown has only 74 priests for 89 parishes.[27]

In the Archdiocese of Chicago, the number of priests dropped from a high of 1,264 in 1980 to 766 in 2015. As priests retire, there are only ten men per year ordained to replace them. As a result, the archdiocese expects to have only 240 priests by 2030.[28]

In the face of these calamitous statistics, Archbishop Blaise Cupich has labeled this vast overhaul of his archdiocese a "renewal" rather than a catastrophe in the making. In light of the chaos and churn this overhaul will cause his flock, his words sound both hollow and misleading.

Not only are there fewer priests, they are also older. According to a CARA report in 2009, the average age of priests in the United

States is 63. Future Church reported that 75 percent of active diocesan priests are over 55. These older priests are also working harder. Significant numbers of priests have been relegated to being Sunday circuit riders.

A brochure issued by the Catholic Foundation of Greater Philadelphia in March of 2016 admitted its own lack of presence in Chester, Pennsylvania, where one in every three citizens lives in poverty. A young priest with only three years of experience under his belt is the pastor of Chester's one remaining parish, an amalgam of several closed parishes. His parish is so large that it includes three exits on Interstate 95. Being pastor, the brochure states, requires "every one of his considerable assets, including his youthful energy, his graduate degree, and his commanding 6'5" physical presence."[29] His parish, St. Katherine Drexel, is "the Catholic center of gravity in Chester." The pastor's "relentless optimism" cannot disguise the fact that that less can never add up to more and that even the most dedicated, energetic, and hardworking priests are often subject to burnout and stress-related illnesses. The archdiocese has sent out four mailings to the faithful in the spring and summer of 2016 asking for money to support the last stand of Catholicism in Chester.

The priest shortage is global. For instance, Brazil's Catholic population of 140 million souls has only 1,800 priests to serve them. The country needs almost ten times more in order to fully function. The lack of priests leads to diminished pastoral care and few numbers of Sunday Masses. The severe shortage of priests is driving Catholics into Pentecostal and evangelical churches.[30]

There are two very obvious ways to keep many parishes open that the bishops have rejected outright as they choose instead to inflict turmoil and disarray on parish communities: first, calling back the thousands of priests who decided to marry and were summarily tossed out of the priesthood; and second, ordaining women. Not to do so further entrenches the hierarchy in a mentality of scarcity while ignoring the blessings that would pour down overflowing into their—and the laity's—laps and solve a good portion of the parish closures.

Sadly, former Pope John Paul II actually found the idea of women priests so repugnant and repellent that he actually forbade Catholics even to talk about it under pain of ecclesiastical sanctions. This policy was carried on by his successor, Benedict XVI, who removed priests and bishops from ministry posthaste with a zeal not shown towards those who had sexually abused children when they mentioned women's ordination—even indirectly. American Maryknoll Father Roy Bourgeois and Irish Redemptorist Father Tony Flannery both lost their status in their respective orders and their faculties to say Mass when they publicly supported the ordination of women. Their faculties have not been restored by Pope Francis.

Benedict also relieved Australian Bill Morris of his position as bishop of the Diocese of Toowoomba in 2011. Morris wrote a pastoral letter in 2006 detailing the severe shortage of ordained, male, celibate priests in Australia and saying that he would be open to the ordination of women if Rome allowed it. In response, Benedict sent Bishop Charles Chaput, who was then the bishop of Denver as an apostolic visitor, that is, inquisitor to sniff out Morris' alleged failure to follow church teachings. Denied permission to view Chaput's conclusion, Morris was summarily removed and offered no recourse to appeal the decision.[31]

The Vatican under Benedict also directed the investigation of women religious orders for alleged support of women's ordination. Many lay people who publicly supported it were either threatened with the loss of their jobs or denied communion. On the other hand, bishops who covered up the sexual abuse of minors were never made the target of a papal investigation, nor were they asked to resign. All continue to receive the Eucharist.

As a result of this obduracy, the ordained, members of religious orders, as well as many members of the laity, remain fearfully silent, a silence that not only aids and abets an unjust practice but also contributes to the next wave of closings as the number of male priests continues to plunge.

Pope Francis, who packages his new wine of mercy in the old wineskins of misogyny, has sadly followed suit, speaking out of both sides of his mouth as he tries to honor women while simultaneously barring them from ministry.

In the summer of 2016, Pope Francis called together a panel to study the possibility of ordaining women to the diaconate. This commission is composed of six women and six men. Two of the women are nuns, and all of the men are ordained priests. The overseer of the commission is an archbishop.

Although the apostle Paul clearly writes of the deacon Phoebe (and the apostle Junia) in his Epistle to the Romans that predates all of the gospels and which all Catholics acknowledge as "the Word of God," Francis remains unconvinced about the legality of women deacons. (The Greek word for deacon that Paul uses is the same word used in Acts 6:4 by Paul to describe the male deacons who preached the Word.) Instead, Francis has fixated upon the question of whether female deacons were ordained in the same manner as the male deacons when in reality, very significant numbers of biblical scholars have made the point repeatedly that Jesus ordained no one in the modern sense in the New Testament. Other scholars, such as Gary Macy and John Wijngaards, have written that in medieval times men and women were ordained as deacons in exactly the same type of ceremony. Francis has ignored all of their research, as he has ignored the presence of inscriptions on fourth-century tombstones that clearly label women as priests and the ancient mosaics of women dressed in liturgical garb holding up bread and wine.

While the commission studies the possibility of women deacons in a group weighted down by clerics who have everything to lose by admitting women to holy orders, Francis continues to support his predecessors' prohibition of women's ordination to the priesthood to the point of claiming that John Paul II has spoken the final word on women's ordination in his 1994 encylical, *Ordinatio Sacerdotalis*. Thus, Francis's call for a "deep theology" of women rings hollow to the ears of many women. A deep theology of women written by women has existed for at least fifty years. Francis has either chosen not to read this truly deep theology of women or he doesn't like it and would prefer one written by clerical men that will, in the end, toe the party line of no women priests, ever.

Faced with ongoing parish mergers and the decreasing number of priests, eleven very brave priests in Cologne, Germany, wrote an open letter stating the obvious about the future of priestly ministry and, by extension, the future of the church:

> We urgently need to forge ahead with courageous initiatives on the question of the admission of women to the priesthood. It makes no sense continuously to ask the Holy Spirit for vocations while at the same time excluding women from priestly ministry.[32]

Research done by the Barna Group in March of 2017 indicates that an overwhelming eighty percent of Catholics support women priests.[33] Seventy-two percent support married male priests.[34] The bishops ignore these statistics at their own peril.

This slash-and-burn policy of closing parishes and disregarding the People of God suggests that the bishops are far more intent on preserving the male priesthood than they are in providing the Eucharist. By placing the continuance of the celibate male clergy above the survival of the Eucharist and, ultimately, the church itself, the hierarchy has diminished its mission, focus, and identity. The Great Commission in Matthew to make disciples of all nations cannot be accomplished by contracting or eliminating the presence of those who would do this.

As Christians, we know that God, our creator, continually makes all things new. Therefore, we should listen to what the divine is saying as the world turns and we move on to another page of history.

The People of God have indicated their willingness to try something new as they follow the Holy Spirit, who always chooses to fix things in unusual and non-traditional ways. As always, the Spirit watches and She waits. There are signs and portents that She is at work now, guiding the daring towards Her new vision of church where all are welcome and all are equal under Her great law of love.

CHAPTER THREE
CONTROL

*"The minister as manager, the pastor as CEO,
the leader as "the authority" are models of church
leadership that are not worthy of the one who
emptied himself and took the form of a servant."*

—Michael W. Foss, Power Surge: Six Marks
of Discipleship for a Changing Church

C losing a parish sows anger and causes enormous pain in the
faithful. Canon (church) lawyer Sister Kate Kuenstler described a bishop's edict to bolt the parish door as a "blunt instru-
ment that endangers faith and causes harm."[1]

Consequently, when parishes are slated to be closed, the first
thing people do is complain. The second thing they do is protest.
The third thing they do is act.

In the early days of parish closings, complaining to your bishop
about his usually unilateral decision brought certain risks. In 1972,
an African American woman described meeting with former Philadelphia Cardinal John Krol at the behest of her fellow parishioners

to request that her parish remain open. The woman, then in her early twenties, recalled being escorted to the cardinal's office by two big, burly men. The cardinal never asked her to sit down. Instead, he told her that if she ever complained about anything again, she would be excommunicated. The terrified young woman was escorted back to the elevator by her guards. Neither she nor any other member of that parish took their complaints any further. St. Teresa of Avila Parish closed without incident.

During the first decade of the twenty-first century, the sexual abuse scandal placed the laity on a more level plane with the once idolized clergy. These now empowered Catholics felt free to stand up to their bishop. Many took their case to Rome in defiance of their bishops to appeal the closures that were made without their input. Many Catholics began claiming that they were the majority members of the church so their voices needed to be respected and heard. The bishops, used to unquestioning obedience, were not happy. While none of these people was excommunicated, their voices were rarely, if ever, heeded by either the bishops or by the pope. Instead, the concerns of devoted people were slapped away as if they were unreasonable demands from whinny teenagers.

When a parish in Boston presented a petition signed by 3,500 people asking to keep their parish open to an archdiocesan official, he replied, "We are not interested in petitions." When asked by a member of the petitioning party what they should do with the petitions, the official replied, "You should just go and fuck yourself."[2]

When members of St. Thomas the Apostle Parish in Boston informed then Bishop Richard Lennon that they were going to appeal to Rome to keep their parish open, Lennon replied, "Don't waste your time."[3]

When parishioners expressed their dismay to Philadelphia's Archbishop Chaput about the closing of their financially solvent parish, one woman described the official answer as being akin to, "Sit down and shut up."[4]

While Our Lady of Peace parishioners in New York continued their desperate attempt to keep their well-attended parish open by entering into a second round of appeals to Rome, Dolan rented out their parish building to the Coptic Orthodox Church right from under them in spite of ongoing negotiations.[5]

In New Orleans, the bishop arranged to have protestors evicted from parishes they had occupied. Two were arrested.

In spite of less-than-pastoral treatment, many people have continued in their efforts to keep their parishes open, refusing to go gently into the void of parish oblivion.

When Bernard Law's successor Richard Lennon began closing parishes in Boston in 2004, two years after the *Boston Globe* exposed both the existence of sexual abuse of children and its cover-up by church leadership, not only did the people revolt, some occupied their parishes in defiance of the bishop.

Occupation by the faithful of St. Frances Cabrini Parish in Scituate, Massachusetts, for thirteen years did not change the mind of Lennon's successor, Sean O'Malley, who according to Papal Nuncio Pietro Sambi had "a mandate from God to guide the church" and needed to be obeyed.[6] Rather than respecting their fortitude and dedication, Cardinal O'Malley took the parishioners to court to force them out. The archdiocesan lawyer labeled the protestors, who regularly held prayer services, "trespassers, subject to arrest" who had no right to be on the property.[7] The lawyer for the archdiocese failed to mention that St. Frances Cabrini sat upon prime real estate worth a couple of million dollars. Our Lady of Good Counsel in East Boston, which had been occupied by parishioners for seven years, had recently sold for three million dollars.

After Lennon moved to Cleveland, he continued to close parishes, blanketing his actions with obfuscation. According to his spokesperson as he announced the closure of fifty parishes, "Bishop Lennon believes strongly that his decision will serve the broad needs of the diocese and create vibrancy for each parish."[8] The people did not agree with his quite obviously untrue assessment. When Lennon tried to preach at a parish slated for closure, the parishioners walked out.

A group called "Keep the Faith in Frankford" organized four years ago because there is now no Catholic parish in the entire Frankford section of Philadelphia, a high-density working-class area with a large Catholic population. Patricia Smiley, the organizer of the group, said that St. Joachim Parish, opened in 1843, had no debt and an income from renting the parish school. The Oblate Order provided a priest. Two hundred souls worshipped there every Sunday. Members of the group gather together almost every Sunday for a prayer service outside of their shuttered church. The group has yet to receive a satisfactory answer from the Archdiocese of Philadelphia as to why their parish was closed. The archbishop has steadfastly refused to meet with them.

The bishop's refusal to meet with traumatized parishioners is not unusual. According to canon lawyer Sister Kate Kuenstler, the parish representatives will wait an eternity for a call from their shepherd. She added that lay people who think they can somehow persuade the bishop to change his mind are having nothing but a pipe dream. Patrick Hildebrandt expressed this hierarchical mentality on his Philadelphia Church Project blog:

> We want to continue to destroy and desecrate the institutions you hold dear. And we don't want anyone who might otherwise hold us accountable to get involved.[9]

Along with complaining, protesting, and acting, Catholics are justifiably sad, upset, and angry when faced with the closure of their beloved parish. They understand that parishes are very important neighborhood entities that provide the means for people to gather in community. A parish is not merely the place for Sunday worship. It's where people are baptized, where they hear the Word broken open every Sunday or perhaps daily. It's the place where people take their dreams, their hopes, and wishes and place them in the heart of God. It's the place where people break bread together and realize their own brokenness. It's a place where people can put themselves back together again in a familiar and comfortable place. It's a place from which people are buried in the midst of the community that nurtured them. It is for these reasons that the closing of a neighborhood church is so personally devastating and hurtful.

While these activities can certainly take place anywhere in any church, Catholics know that this is not so simple. There is a deep and abiding attachment to a place that one's ancestors built or where one's own parents and grandparents were baptized, married, and buried. There is comfort and a sense of belonging when looking at the stained-glass windows each week or seeing the same faces in the same pews each week. This experience is called community, a fragile, beautiful thing that takes years to build and many hours of painstaking work to sustain. To the bishops, on the other hand, one parish is like another and, like a priest, is an interchangeable part that gets moved around at the bishops' discretion.

In spite of the intense feelings of parishioners, the vast majority of parishes close without incident. As the priest and money shortage becomes more acute, more and more parishes will slip into oblivion, their stories, their histories, their stained-glass windows, their organs, their sculptures, and their people lost to history. Forty percent of the people in these congregations never again belong to a Catholic parish.[10] These traumatized, hurting people were described by Philadelphia's Bishop Chaput as "imaginary losses" and by Providence's Bishop Tobin as both lacking faith and failing to appreciate the sacred.

Peter Borre who, like Kuenstler has helped parishioners petition Rome to keep their parishes open, stated fatalistically in his blog, "No parish is safe. It means under financial duress, any bishop can appropriate any parish."[11]

Kuenstler wrote that one of the most obvious outcomes of parish suppression was additional money in diocesan coffers as the parishes, often on prime real estate, were sold off to the highest bidder.

Deacon Tom Croker, director of property services for the Archdiocese of Philadelphia, proved Borre and Kuenstler's point. While commenting uncomprehendingly on the fact that people get "emotional" when their parish is closed or sold, Croker said the sale of church property—over parishioner protests—brings in much-needed revenues to an organization in "dire straits."[12] Income from the sale of property thus trumps the good will and unique needs of the flock.

It shouldn't have to be this way. There are ways to keep many parishes open, in spite of the fact that a bishop has declared it dead.

According to church reform organization Future Church, parishes should not be allowed to close at the behest of a bishop, because each parish is a community of faith that "once formed and recognized, becomes a '"juridic person,' which by nature is perpetual unless it is legitimately suppressed or stops all activity for a 100 years."[13] Canon Law reads, "The salvation of souls, which must always be the supreme law in the Church, is to be kept before one's eyes."[14]

In her "Commentary on Vatican Decrees Upholding Cleveland Parish Appeals," Sister Kate Kuenstler lists four non-legitimate reasons to close parishes:

1. The shortage of priests.
2. The church is in close proximity to another church.
3. The church is no longer considered necessary for worship when a parish is suppressed or merged.
4. The maintenance of a building no longer needed as a church for Divine worship is a financial burden to the parish.[15]

Sister Christine Schenk, former director of Future Church, has described a parish as, "A living organism. It should not just be summarily broken up for financial reasons or because of a shortage of priests."[16] In other words, bishops should not be declaring parishes dead before exhausting every single possibility of resuscitation.

Kuenstler expressed the pain of the people of the Diocese of Cleveland. These sentiments are shared by all Catholics faced with the demise of their parish:

> The pain caused by this restructuring, and subsequently imposed upon the parishioners of the Diocese of Cleveland is something that needs to be seriously addressed. The tragedy of this matter exists in how many souls have already been affected. The Congregation for Clergy identified the grave cause in the Bishop's error, but what is of extreme gravity is the woundedness of the people of the Diocese of Cleveland. Such imprudent decision-making scarred the parishioners deeply and violated the sacred trust relationship that people desire in Episcopal leadership and his trusted advisors. It is not surprising that the parishioners of the Diocese of Cleveland have lost their confidence in the Bishop of Cleveland. The decisions to be made now will either open the door for healing to begin, or drive the parishioners into further isolation for generations to come. Will it be a time for healing? Will it be a time of greater destruction? The answer lies in the authentic recommendations that the Presbyteral Council will provide to the Bishop; and his ability to not just hear, but to truly listen, in order to make a prudent, last and best judgment, in what is the right thing to do for the Salvation of the Souls, and the overall good of the Church of Cleveland.[17]

As mass closures of parishes occur across the country and in Europe, it should be clear to the faithful that there needs to be an alternative to their hand-wringing and capitulating attitude in the face of the alleged power of the bishops who continue to demand obedience and respect while stonewalling their own people with pious platitudes or heaping them with criticism. The People of God should, therefore, plan with urgency for a drastically different way of being and doing church—without the bishops—even if it means that they need to break church law.

The gospels and Pauline Epistles providentially supply Catholics with a basis to act *contra legem*, that is, against church law. Jesus, who lived among the poor in captive Israel, repeatedly told people to desist from the practice of slavish obedience to rules that prevented the full flourishing of every human being. Jesus healed sick people on the Sabbath in direct violation of the law and often took religious authorities to task for their hypocrisy in falling short of the law of love. As Jesus proved by his life and his death, a Christian must be willing to act *contra legem*, that is, against the law, whenever religious or political laws harm individuals within the Body of Christ.

Paul, the self-described zealous Pharisee who followed the letter of the law, learned to his dismay as he lay blinded by a bolt of light that knocked him from his horse that instead of serving God, his violent persecution of the followers of Jesus for breaking the law actually harmed Emmanuel, God with us. Thus, Paul had to break the law he had written upon his heart as a youth, the law that sustained him in adulthood in order to love God more abundantly and become the person that God wanted him to be. Paul removed circumcision as an entry requirement for non-Jews who wished to follow Jesus. For Paul, all things were lawful if they worked for the greater glory of God.

We also know that Jesus did not preach his vision to the powerful religious operatives in Jerusalem because he knew that they, like most dominant people in history, would not willingly cede their power to accommodate the domination free kingdom of God. Instead, Jesus preached the kingdom of God on earth to the poor— whom he commissioned as agents of change. Thus, Jesus regarded the wretched of the earth as prime players in his realm: shepherds, farmers, children, the sick and the suffering, oppressed women, and even those the powerful considered sinners and heretics. He declared the poor, the persecuted, and the marginalized blessed rather than the wealthy, who Mary said in the Magnificat would be taken down from their thrones. It is this ragtag group of poor Palestinian peasants rather than any priestly caste that grew the Jesus movement into a new faith and eventually brought the good news of the Kingdom of God to every part of the world.

Along with scripture, *Lumen Gentium*, the Dogmatic Constitution on the Church, also empowers people to act in God's name. In *Lumen Gentium*, the church clearly proclaims that the people share in Christ's kingly, prophetic, and priestly roles. The document states specifically that Christ, as high priest, has established the People of God as "a kingdom and priests to God... consecrated as a spiritual house and a holy priesthood" in order that they might proclaim the power of God. (LG10)

Even more importantly, the rights of Catholics are guaranteed by canon law. According to canon lawyer Father James Coriden, the 1983 Code of Canon Law can be regarded as having constitutional status to the point of providing Catholics with a "Bill of Rights."[18]

1. The fundamental equality of all Christians, based upon baptism, regarding the right and freedom to cooperate in building up the Body of Christ.
2. The right to petition, that is, to make known to pastors one's needs and hopes.
3. The right to recommend, the right to advise pastors regarding the good of the church, and to participate in public opinion and informing the faithful.
4. The right to receive the Word of God and the sacraments from pastors.
5. The right to participate in worship in accordance with legitimate norms of one's own rite.
6. The right to one's proper spirituality.

7. The right to association; the right to found and direct associations with charitable purposes as an expression of Christian vocation.

8. The right to assembly; the right to hold meetings for the same purpose as to associate.

9. The right to promote the apostolate and to one's own proper initiative in apostolic work, based on the right to participate in the church's mission.

10. The right to Christian education.

11. The right to academic freedom.

12. The freedom to choose one's station in life.

13. The right to a good name and reputation.

14. The right to privacy; the right to have others respect what is intimate to one's self.

15. The right to vindicate one's rights in church court and to defend one's rights in church court with equity and in accordance to the law.

16. The right to be judged.

17. The right to legality regarding sanctions, that is, the right to expect the church to impose sanctions only in accordance to the law.[19]

Theologians since Vatican II have also fleshed out the rights of the laity. Bernard Haring described the availability of the Eucharist as a right: "The people of God have a God-given right to the Eucharist. On the basis of human law, to deprive the people of God of the Eucharist is, objectively, gravely sinful."[20]

Catholics are, then, empowered by scripture, church doctrines, and many theologians in their efforts to preserve their parish community from death by ecclesiastical decree. Thus, keeping a parish open by virtue of the power invested in the People of God is not disobedience but rather common sense. As the history of Christianity—indeed of the world—demonstrates, change almost always comes from the bottom up, from the lived reality of people rather than from the grand claims of power from the men at the top who allege divinely infused power.

Although change can be fearful, disorienting, and even risky, it eventually becomes the new reality. Denying the fact that a situation can be changed or is in the process of changing neither slows down nor prevents change. The growth and development of human beings rather proves this point. We can never deny the fact that our small, loving, cuddly children at some point will morph into sometimes surly, disobedient teenagers with minds of their own or that our youthful vigor will give way to a more sedentary middle age.

Unfortunately, the change inherent in all forms, including the church, eludes the hierarchy of the church, whose members continue to rely upon ancient Greek philosophy of unchanging forms rather than the gospel, life experiences in the world, or the faith life of its people as the basis for their actions.

This Greek philosophy known as Platonism, named after the ancient Greek Plato, is a theory of eternal, perfect, and ideal forms such as beauty, truth, and good that are invisible, unchanging, and imperishable. In this system, which the church adopted with little nuance, the visible was changeable and perishable, if not downright sinful, because it could not be trusted. The church has viewed itself throughout history as an ideal form of good, unchanged from its inception during apostolic times and incapable of being corrupted by culture, history, or even sin. Human experience, on the other hand, lies squarely within the degraded, perishable world awash in secularism and culture and cannot be trusted to produce good.

A world sustained by a theological system of unchanging ideas fits in well with a group of men who fear and resist any type of change and who place themselves on a plane far above the people they are supposed to shepherd by virtue of their membership in this ideal, uncorrupted entity. With heads and hearts deeply buried in an ancient philosophical system that can only look backwards to an ideal world that in fact never actually existed, the bishops have failed to notice the profound shift in consciousness that has changed the world into a very different place. This new world rejects the assertion that ideal, uncorrupted, and thus untouchable institutions can exist or ever existed, while not rejecting what history or tradition can offer. This new world does not, however, cast off idealism and the optimistic belief that good can, indeed, come from change, or the possibility that some things must die in order to be reborn as something else.

It has become imperative for the People of God to orchestrate the change that the hierarchy rejects if their parishes are to survive. By the power invested in ordinary Catholics by God there is no reason to take the bishop's decision to close a parish as either valid or necessary. Every member of the People of God has a role in keeping their own parish alive, with or without the bishop's permission. It is time for the People of God to stop pretending that "Father knows best." It is also time to acknowledge that men whose every need is provided by the laity need to be accountable to the people who keep them housed in fancy mansions, clothed in expensive vestments, and fed with the finest victuals.

In light of the upcoming massive and ongoing parish closings, that time is now.

CHAPTER FOUR
THE DRAGON'S GAME

*"Domination is a contaminant, a disease,
that once introduced, will inexorably spread
throughout the system of societies."*

—*Walter Wink,* Engaging the Powers

A s you prepare to keep your parish open after your bishop has declared it dead, he will probably become one of your harshest critics. He might even excommunicate you or say that you excommunicated yourself by your actions that fly in the face of his authority. As those who are dedicated to keeping their parish alive make their resurrection plans, it is important to know how the role of bishop has changed over the years from being the shepherd of the flock who tenderly cares for all to becoming absolute ruler who sincerely believes that he is in charge of your salvation. It is equally important not to feel daunted by any exercise of ecclesiastical power.

Here is a bit of ancient and modern history.

The church, including both clerics and the laity, never existed in a vacuum. While Christianity originated in Palestine and was based upon the Jewish faith, it grew up in a Hellenic (Greek) world and was profoundly affected by Greek philosophy, as mentioned in the last chapter. After making its way through what is now Greece, Turkey, and North Africa, Christianity then spread to the capital city of the Roman Empire, where in 313 CE the Emperor Constantine declared it to be the religion of the empire, thus enmeshing church with state. After the Bishop of Rome moved into the Lateran Palace, the church took on many of the accoutrements of its Roman patrons: its law, governance style, and its dress, which included wearing the insignia of royalty such as a special headgear, which became known as the miter. Imperial dignity entitled bishops to a throne and a greeting in church that included lighted candles, trumpet blasts, incense, and a choir singing a welcome. Worshippers genuflected before the enthroned bishop and kissed his foot as they entered church.[1]

As the church filled the vacuum left by the fall of the Roman Empire in the fifth century CE, the Bishop of Rome became known as the Pontifex Maximus, a title borrowed from the polytheism practiced by Rome to describe the most important person in the Roman priesthood. By the year 800 CE, the pope had become a kingmaker, crowning Charlemagne the Holy Roman Emperor. Like any political absolute ruler, the Pontifex Maximus Boniface could declare five centuries later, "Every human creature is to be subject to the Roman pontiff." The pope and, by extension, the bishops could now command absolute obedience from their subjects. Compliance with episcopal decrees was enforced by the state.

Linking Jesus with the imperial culture of the time harmonized the power of empire and its trappings of authority with the Christian faith. It also led to a Christology of power with Jesus being perceived as the universal law giver and great judge who demanded absolute obedience from unworthy believers. Jesus' warning that his followers could not serve both God and wealth began to fall on episcopal ears that were becoming more attuned to trumpet blasts announcing their arrival in a place of worship where they sat upon thrones.

Ignatius of Antioch wrote the textbook on ecclesiastical authority in the second century CE. His elevation of the bishop's status to supreme diocesan ruler meant that Christians throughout the centuries began to conflate the office of bishop with the divine. This resulted in the infantilizing of the laity. This idea is confirmed in Ignatius' letter to the Smyrnaeans where he directed his fellow Christians to follow their bishop as Jesus did the Father. Ignatius' opinion of the bishop—that is, of himself—was so high that he believed that the laity who obeyed their bishop were actually obeying God. Consequently, a disobedient parishioner risked his or her salvation.

> See that you all follow the bishop, even as Jesus Christ does the Father, and the presbytery as you would the apostles; and reverence the deacons, as being the institution of God. Let no man do anything connected with the Church without the bishop.... Wherever the bishop shall appear, there let the multitude of the people also be, even as wherever Jesus Christ is, there is the Catholic Church... Whatsoever [the bishop] shall approve of, that is also pleasing to God, so that everything that is done may be secure and valid.... It is well to reverence both God and the bishop. He who honors the bishop has been honored by God; he who does anything without the knowledge of the bishop, does, in reality, serve the devil.[2]

This belief led to the idea that the elevated position of bishop places him at the tip of a theological pyramid next to God, the Creator of heaven and earth, whose divine Hands are then tied to this very human model. In the Ignatian model followed by many modern bishops, only the existence of the bishop allows the safe passage of grace to those below; hence, their elevated status, symbolized by the episcopal ring, the miter, the throne, the golden and brocaded vestments, and the title, "Your Eminence," as well as the claim of some to know the mind and will of God. Because the bishops believe that they are the direct successors of the apostles who created this ideal, uncontaminated church, their sins, though many, have been in the past easily forgiven by themselves, by their fellow bishops, by the pope, and, up until the advent of the sexual abuse scandal, by their flocks.

With this type of history, it must be acknowledged that for lay members to develop a plan to keep a parish afloat in the face of a bishop's directive to close can be frightening. Catholics have been taught that the bishop of a diocese is the point of unity. The bishops themselves have taught that the laity should conform their consciences to episcopal teaching. The expectation of perfect obedience does not encourage lay independence.

The People of God should remember that the reality of the office of bishop differs from these great expectations. History teaches us that instead of being a source of divine grace, many bishops over the centuries have been sources of disunity and downright chaos, as they are today. In the past, some bishops have served as temporal rulers, harshly taxing their subjects, often in absentia. Others have declared war that caused armies to invade the territory of fellow Christians for spurious reasons. Many live on an economic level that is far removed from the vast majority of their flocks. Often, many of them have rejected almost every effort to move humanity forward, from actively opposing religious freedom to agreeing with the banning of birth control, even when mothers were dying and families starving, to supporting slavery. Recently and most egregiously, far too many have ignored and covered up child sexual abuse. Thus, the office of bishop has often fallen to the lowest common denominator in their respective societies, all the while claiming that as representatives of the ideal "spotless bride of Christ" they are immune from a culture that taints everyone but themselves.

Bishops are, of course, mere men who, like all other human beings, have fallen short of the glory of God. Ordination does not provide a shield against sin or confer ability, wisdom, or authority. The ontological change that clerics believe they undergo at ordination does not automatically make priests kinder, gentler, smarter, wiser, or faithful. It does not by default mold them into good preachers or wise shepherds. Ignatius of Antioch, a man of his second-century times, was incorrect in his lofty assessment of the office of bishop. He thought much too highly of himself and other men. For twenty-first century people to continue to believe that in obeying a mere man one is obeying God is idolatry.

If your bishop accuses you of sin as you work to resurrect the parish he has declared dead, it is important for you to be aware of and to remind him of the presence of ecclesiastical sin. Below are several egregious examples.

Former Kansas City Archbishop Robert Finn did not have the decency to resign his position after he was convicted of a misdemeanor for failing to report a priest who had child pornography on his computer. John Nienstedt of the Twin Cities claimed in 2012 that his position as bishop was like that of the paterfamilias rather than that of a CEO of a company and thus could not resign after the diocese was charged with failing to protect children under his watch.

Mark L. Bartchak and his predecessor Joseph Adamec, current and former bishops of Altoona/Johnstown Diocese in Pennsylvania, both allowed Joseph Maurizio to remain in ministry for five years after the priest had been reported to the diocese for sexually abusing boys at a Honduran orphanage in 2009. Disturbed by the priest's ongoing visits to Central America and coupled with the diocese's lack of interest in pursuing the allegations, the charity that ran the orphanage reported the situation to BishopAccountabilty.org, an organization that documents the sexual abuse crisis in the Catholic Church. Bishop Accountability shared the charity's concerns with a lawyer with ties to the U.S. Department of Justice and with the Department of Homeland Security. Only when agents began investigating Maurizio did Bartchak remove him from ministry.

Anne Barrett Doyle of Bishop Accountability commented on both bishops' "total lack of interest" in Maurizio's behavior.[3]

Robert Carlson, the Archbishop of St. Louis, stated under oath that he did not know if the sexual abuse of children was a crime.[4]

In January of 2015, a priest in Palm Beach, Florida, was locked out of his parish and vilified online by his bishop, Gerald Barbarito. Barbarito had directed the priest to put a visiting priest who was showing pornography to a fourteen-year-old boy on a plane back to India rather than reporting him to the police. Neither Cardinal Sean O'Malley, who was sent to Palm Beach fifteen years previously to clean up a mess left by a former Palm Beach bishop and who sits on the papal sex abuse commission, nor the Vatican stepped in to help the priest.[5]

These are but six of the many American prelates who failed Shepherding 101 and refused to accept responsibility for their actions after the Charter for the Protection of Children and Young People with their "zero tolerance" policy had been adopted by the U.S. bishops. Very few of their brother bishops or fellow priests have taken Finn, Nienstedt, Adamec, Carlson, Barbarito, or Bartchak publicly to task for their egregious lapses. Nor have priests in their respective dioceses. Sadly, vows of obedience far too often replace moral courage.

Neither John Paul II nor Benedict XVI made any move to remove bishops who have engaged in the egregious cover-up of child abuse. In fact, some were rewarded. Bernard Law, a former archbishop of Boston who covered up grievous crimes against children, was rewarded for his efforts by being named the archpriest of the Basilica of Santa Maria Maggiore in Rome by John Paul II. He is also the cardinal priest of Saint Susanna, the American Catholic Church in Rome. People still kiss his ring and call him, "Your Eminence."[6]

John Paul II turned a blind eye towards the notorious pedophile Marcial Maciel Degollado, founder of the Legionaries of Christ. Maciel, a prodigious fund-raiser who donated vast amounts of money to the Vatican, envisioned a return to a pre–Vatican II church, a vision shared by John Paul II. Despite receiving letters from seminarians as far back as the late 1970s carefully documenting Maciel's ongoing sexual abuse and drug use, John Paul II called him "an efficacious guide to youth." While Benedict as Cardinal Ratzinger, prefect of the Confraternity of Christian Doctrine, conducted witch hunts against theologians who seemed to deviate from the Vatican company line, he permitted Maciel to remain "Nuestro Padre" or "Our Father," as he taught his followers to call him until he stepped down as head of the order in 2006. In spite of his crimes against between twenty and a hundred seminarians, some as young as twelve, and fathering at least three children with two different women, Maciel was permitted to comfortably retire to a life of prayer and penance by Benedict XVI.[7] On the other hand, priests like Roy Bourgeois and Tony Flannery who voiced support for women's ordination found themselves without faculties and financial support almost instantaneously after making their unorthodox opinions known.

Francis' track record is but little improved in the area of bishop discipline. In the early days of his papacy, Józef Wesolowski, papal nuncio in the Dominican Republic, was spirited out of that country by the Vatican on the eve of his trial for child abuse and the possession of large amounts of child pornography. While he was laicized the following year, he was not imprisoned and was seen walking freely around the streets of Vatican City as if in a "golden cage," according to the Latin Times. Wesolowski died in 2015 on the eve of his Vatican-run trial.[8]

In 2015, Francis elevated Juan Barros to bishop even though the Chilean people believed Barros to be complicit in covering up child abuse. Francis dismissed their protests as complaints from a "bunch of 'leftists.'"[9]

To his credit, Francis did establish a commission to study and combat the abuse of children and vulnerable adults. The commission, however, was plagued from the beginning by a lack of office space, staff, and supplies and, most importantly, by the Roman Curia's lack of cooperation. When Irish citizen and commission member Marie Collins resigned in despair from the commission on March 1, 2017, she asked, "Is this reluctance [to implement recommendations] driven by internal politics, fear of change, clericalism which instills a belief that 'they know best' or a closed mindset which sees abuse as an inconvenience or a clinging to old institutional attitudes?" In a statement written for the *National Catholic Reporter*, Collins compared the "fine words" spoken in public about the horror of sexual abuse with "contrary actions behind closed doors" where the clerical members of the commission refused to cooperate.[10]

In spite of these very unpleasant facts, which testify to the fact that they are just like everyone else, the bishops do not take kindly to parishioners who stray from episcopal insistence on obedience and may level charges of disunity upon those whose opinions they choose to ignore. In spite of this, Catholics should not fear upsetting or antagonizing their bishop. Both the Old and the New Testaments urge those who contemplate a difficult move not to fear as they move in a different direction. In fact, the divine counsel "Do not fear" is the most repeated and important message in all of scripture, as freedom from fear confers extraordinary power upon those who refuse to be mastered by it. The next chapters will describe what can happen when parishioners act independently and fearlessly.

In addition, as many church reformers like to say, the church is not the bishops or the pope. The church is the People of God. As discussed earlier, the People of God have a right to take matters into their own hands, especially when their survival as a community is at stake.

In spite of the empowerment given to Catholics at their baptism, those who would plan a challenge to the bishop should prepare to protect themselves with the full armor of God to shield themselves from the slings and arrows sure to be launched by both the ecclesiastical powers and perhaps by some of their fellow Catholics who will disagree with them and side with the bishop. They should pray often and remember to keep their eyes on the prize—the survival of their parish community.

The reality is that in spite of fulminations from a bishop and possible threats of excommunication, nothing can ever separate anyone from the love of God. As Paul wrote in Romans 8:38, "And I am convinced that nothing can ever separate us from God's love. Neither death nor life, neither angels nor demons, neither our fears for today nor our worries about tomorrow—not even the powers of hell can separate us from God's love." And neither can the local bishop. In the end, this move is not about a bishop's feelings or his power or his opinion. It is about the resurrection of a parish community.

As you, the reader, plan ways to keep your parish community open against the expressed intention of your bishop, remember Jesus, who is the reason you are even reading this book. At the very outset of his ministry, Jesus proclaimed to those assembled that he was consecrated by God to bring good news to poor people, to proclaim release to captives, to restore sight to the blind, to set the oppressed at liberty, and to proclaim a year of favor from the Lord.[11] He announced this at his local synagogue to people who knew him, grew up with him, and played with him in the dusty streets of Nazareth. His fellows in the village were neither impressed nor excited by his declaration. In fact, they thought he was crazy. His fellow villagers, his friends, and perhaps his relatives, drove him out of town asking, "Isn't this the carpenter's son?" Just who did Jesus think he was?

There will be those who will ask you the same question as you prepare to keep your parish open. How dare you? Who do you think you are? Your bishop has spoken.

The reality is that you have seen and felt what the bishops refuse to see and cannot feel as they sit upon their thrones in the cathedral far away from the lives of their flock. You know personally that the closing of parishes diminishes the presence of God in your neighborhoods. It dashes your hopes and dampens your faith. It often breaks your hearts.

You are the People of God. The bishops cannot exist without you. Take heart. Jesus, our Emmanuel, God with us, lives among the People of God. He promised that He would be with you until the end of time. Indeed, He will.

CHAPTER FIVE
THE CRACK

"What breach in our walls comes with their coming, to let into our prison the smell of sun and grass? Their existence tells itself through the crack. One such was Jesus the Jew. Let him pass."

—Sheila Moon

On its website, Future Church provides a template for appealing to the Vatican to keep parishes open. Thus far, Future Church has helped thirteen parishes in Cleveland and thirty-six parishes in eight other dioceses win their appeal to remain open. Many other parishes, have not been so fortunate. The Vatican inevitably supports their man in the miter over the people who pay for it. The bishop is the prince in his own diocese, so the Vatican does not often circumvent his decisions even as one parish after another closes and faith stumbles.

Some dioceses do try to keep some parishes open by appointing lay leaders who are empowered to baptize, bury, and organize Sunday communion services with hosts pre-consecrated by a circuit-riding priest. However, many parishioners have indicated that a church without an active Eucharistic celebration quickly becomes unsatisfactory. Dissatisfaction leads to a decrease in attendance. A decrease in attendance soon leaves the parish on the chopping block.

Before despairing, those who wish to continue to keep their parishes open should know that there are church communities that were designated for closure by their bishops and were able to remain open. Not only have they survived ecclesiastical onslaughts, they have also thrived.

Corpus Christi in Rochester, New York, was the first to throw down the gauntlet. While not closed by the bishop, the parish packed up its bags and reformed in 1998 as Spiritus Christi, taking 1,100 parishioners and all of their considerable ministries with them after Bishop Matthew Clark transferred popular pastor Jim Callan for allowing a woman, Mary Ramerman, to stand at the altar with him wearing an alb, the symbol of priesthood. Clark did this in spite of Callan's bursting-at-the-seams services and stellar record of providing services to the poor. Spiritus Christi, which is not under the aegis of the Diocese of Rochester, is now the largest parish in the entire city of Rochester, New York. On the other hand, Corpus Christi was clustered with three other parishes. Three out of the four have now closed down.

According to their website, Spiritus Christi is based upon two scriptural pillars: "No one who comes to me will I ever reject," and "I have come to bring good news to the poor, free the prisoners, and liberate the oppressed."

Their mission statement reads: "We are a Christ-centered Catholic community reaching beyond the institutional church to be inclusive of all. Jesus Christ is our Pastor; therefore we open our church as a spiritual refuge. We hold the Eucharist as the center of our sacramental life. We embrace the challenge of the scriptures. We are ordinary people joyously celebrating the opportunity to follow Jesus' radical message of unconditional love." The parish has consistently maintained its mission to the poor. It has also maintained its dedication to transparency and parish-wide decision making.

Spiritus Christi has 1,500 members, 33 full- and part-time staff, and an operating budget of $1.7 million dollars. Eleven hundred parishioners attend Mass every Sunday.[1]

Church of St. Stephen parish in Minneapolis was reborn after Vatican II as a peace and justice church. Like Spiritus Christi, St. Stephen's began a multitude of ministries to serve the poor, the sick, and the suffering. The liturgy changed over the course of these years to reflect both their mission to the poor and the changes inspired by Vatican II.

Thus, the pulpit was opened up to members of the laity, including women, to broaden perspectives and share the wisdom of multiples lives. Members of the community were also asked for their input on the readings after the homily. The community eschewed sexist language and prayed to God, our Mother and Father. The priest/presider sat in the pews with the congregation rather than upon a raised chair because of the belief in the equality of all people before God. The community refused to use vessels made of precious metals because they preferred spending money on the poor.

In February of 2008, Archbishop Flynn gave St. Stephen's three weeks to conform to the guidelines outlined in the General Instruction on the Roman Missal, which would eliminate their use of nonsexist language. They were directed to discontinue a beloved Sunday 9 a.m. prayer service because it caused "confusion" and "pain" for some members. They were told that their new pastor, a young man of thirty-four with only a few years of experience under his belt, would become the undisputed liturgical leader.

Faced with what they considered to be hierarchical directives designed to ensure a conformity that did not reflect the mission of their beloved community, the majority of the members of St. Stephen decided to leave and have their Sunday celebration elsewhere saying: "We are committed to the future of a Catholic Church that builds loving, inclusive, prayerful, justice-serving communities of faith. We must move away from a culture of clerical power, control, privilege and secrecy. We are not against authority. We are against patriarchy, which disrespects people. Unity is not uniformity."[2]

Archbishop Flynn's ultimatum led 350 families to leave the Church of St. Stephen. Two hundred or so reformed as the Spirit of St. Stephen's Catholic Community, which meets in another site and functions as a parish apart from the Archdiocese of Minneapolis and St. Paul. Collections are down by 90% at the diocesan Church of St. Stephen, where the young pastor told a reporter that he has great hopes for renewal with the couple of dozen people who remain.[3]

The Community of St. Peter formed in 2010 after Cleveland Bishop Richard Lennon decided to close what one parishioner described as "the crown jewel" of Cleveland, St. Peter Catholic Church. She wrote that the liturgy at St. Peter's was "vibrant and prayerful." The Eucharist was celebrated "in an elegant way."[4] Instead of closing, Pastor Robert Marrone and 350 former parishioners leased space in a nearby facility; secured a new altar, baptismal font, and new icons; and continued to operate as the Community of St. Peter, albeit under different circumstances. They now operate as a fully functioning parish without the permission of Cleveland's bishop, Richard Lennon.

Lennon claimed in 2010 that St. Peter's broke "unity and communion" with the wider church by reforming into their own parish. Falling back upon an inflated understanding of the position of bishop, Lennon said that being a member of St. Peter's affects one's relationship with the Lord, clearly ignoring the fact that adult Catholics are, indeed, quite capable of having their own relationship with Jesus without the bishop's permission. Sadly, like far too many of the nation's bishops, Lennon would rather engage in condemnation rather than dialogue.

Members of the Community of St. Peter, however, perceive themselves as traditional Catholics who decided to act on their own rather than allow the bishop to close their community. They have not challenged the tenets of their faith, in spite of the bishop's condemnation.

According to parishioner Bob Zack, "We consider ourselves neither a focal point of dissent nor a schismatic organization.... The bishop says the church is his real estate. Fine. Take it. We have no control over that. But we have decided to keep our community together. We believe, as the bishop has repeatedly stated, that we as Catholics, not any particular church building, are the church... I have a hard time understanding why we need the bishop's permission for us to worship together."

In the same article, Norbert Koehn, the sculptor who made the new altar and baptismal font said, "This is a new beginning, a new start. It has nothing to do with the bishop anymore."

As for any attempt at excommunication, Koehn said, "I don't think that once you've been baptized it can be taken away from you by anybody."

According to *The Plain Dealer*, the Community of St. Peter has a budget of $200,000 per year.[5]

St. Stanislaus Kostka Polish Catholic Parish had an agreement with the Archdiocese of St. Louis that dated back to the nineteenth century. The bishop would appoint the priests, but the parish would retain ownership of the property and assets. When the archdiocese tried to move St. Stanislaus' assets of over 8 million dollars into a diocesan fund in 2003, the parishioners rebelled and refused to turn over the money. Archbishop Burke then retaliated by removing the diocesan priests from the parish, ending all celebrations of the Eucharist.[6]

The advisory board of St. Stanislaus then hired Father Marek Bozek as their pastor and continued to celebrate Mass and the sacraments. Burke retaliated by excommunicating both Bozek and the board of trustees. When the court finally awarded the property and assets to the parish of St. Stanislaus in 2012, Burke's successor, Robert Carlson, pledged to fight the decision all the way to the Supreme Court.[7] Today, St. Stanislaus remains alive and well in spite of fulminations from three bishops. Each Sunday, between two and three hundred people gather for worship.

Thirty-five years ago, the local bishop tried to close down St. Dominic Parish in Amsterdam in the Netherlands. Directed to resurrect a dying parish, the pastor, Jan Nieuwenhuis, was willing to try almost anything to keep the parish open and his parishioners fed. Unlike his bishops, Nieuwenhuis realized that the time was fast approaching when there would not be enough priests in the Netherlands to provide the Eucharist to the number of Catholics who lived there, in spite of the foreign priests harvested from priest plantations in Africa and India, a policy that left those very needy areas without their native born priests. Anticipating the inevitable, he took steps to ensure that the Eucharist would be available to the people in his parish. He did this by developing a theology "from below" that recognized the many and varied gifts within his own community.

Under Nieuwenhuis' guidance, non-ordained members of the community approved by the community, regularly preside and preach at Mass. The co-pastor is a woman. Because of Nieuwenhuis' vision and faith in God to make all things new, St. Dominic has flourished. Currently, St. Dominic Parish packs the church with 600 people every Sunday and has 3,000 people on the rolls. It is the only growing Catholic parish in the Netherlands.

Nieuwenhuis, along with several other Dutch Dominicans, published a thirty-four page booklet in 2007 entitled *Church and Ministry*. This document is a must-read for all who intend to keep their parish alive since it provides the theology and rationale behind the establishment of intentional Eucharistic communities and exposes the danger inherent in restricting the celebration of the Eucharist to priests in a priest-poor environment that will only get worse with time. For the Dutch Dominicans, the availability, indeed, the very survival of the Eucharist as a form of Catholic worship far surpasses the current requirement for a male, celibate priesthood. The document recommends that, given the acute nature of the priest shortage, it has become both necessary and common sense for parish communities to designate theologically trained non-ordained members of good character to preside at the Eucharist in their own parish in order to keep it open.

The document is revolutionary on many levels. Aside from calling for non-ordained presiders, the authors also call for a modernization of liturgical language and for the congregation to pray the words of institution along with the presider as what they call a "conscious declaration of faith."[8]

The men, all priests who remain in good standing, wrote what many reformers believe: current church law reserving the priesthood to unmarried men is based upon an antiquated notion of human sexuality and an "outdated philosophy of humankind."[9] According to Robert McClory and the Dutch authors, this plan is a blueprint for those who would establish small, Eucharistic communities in lieu of the big parishes that are being closed. The Dominicans believe that without the existence of these small communities, the Eucharist will not be preserved as the Catholic Church's central act of worship.

The transition from being an approved diocesan parish with bishop-appointed priests to being declared in schism and excommunicated was not easy for any of the people involved in these parishes. (While not in schism, St. Dominic is an ecumenical parish.) Many parishioners could not bring themselves to commit what they believed to be disobedience and choose to remain in diocesan sponsored churches. In some cases, animosity grew between those who made the move and those who remained. Writs of excommunication dripped from the pens of bishops while epithets like "apostates" flew from some mouths.

In spite of Jesus' admonition to forgive seventy times seven, hard feelings remain. Thirteen years after the formation of Spiritus Christi, the Diocese of Rochester still harbored a grudge and refused to speak about the break-away parish to reporter Michael O'Malley. Instead, the diocese responded in an email, "We are not in communion with Spiritus Christi and do not want to comment."[10]

In addition to sometimes very harsh criticism from church leaders and former fellow parishioners, the people of Spiritus Christi, St. Stephen, and St. Peter had to leave their beloved parish building and move into new surroundings. This transition was difficult but in the end proved to be life-giving, as the parish relocated and re-formed. The important point is that people felt empowered to make their own decisions to ensure their survival without the permission of their respective bishops, who had not only failed them, but disowned them as well.

Those who wonder if preserving these parishes was worth the ensuing dissention need to consult with the hundreds of people who happily and faithfully attend Mass each Sunday in their new communities and who have pledged their lives, their time, and their livelihoods to make their new parish work, albeit under somewhat different circumstances.

The good news is that the Holy Spirit is alive, well, and, indeed, thriving in these new communities. The Spirit called Shekinah in the Hebrew Bible simply cannot be contained, retrained, restrained, explained, or maintained by men or by women. God is wild, holy fire, "shook foil," according to poet Gerard Manley Hopkins. Peter, like the prophet Joel, and later Augustine tried and failed to describe the incomprehensible nature of God, who pours out God's Spirit upon the less-than-usual suspects—without anyone's permission. Before Joshua, the successor of Moses, understood the depth and breadth and height of God's power, he bitterly complained to Moses about undesignated people prophesizing in the name of God. Jesus received a similar complaint from his disciples when they tried to restrict something Jesus wanted poured out and overflowing into everyone's laps. Jesus, like Moses, dismissed out of hand the idea of human-controlled parceling out of God's power because the power of God simply cannot be limited by man-made laws.

Thus, the Spirit has a way of making Her will known, even to those who have closed up their ears and hardened their hearts to Her voice. That new way forward is the establishment of small, intentional Eucharistic communities designed by and for the People of God. The People of God who build new communities follow the advice of Pope Francis, who has urged Catholics to, "Find new ways to spread the Word of God to every corner of the world."

CHAPTER SIX
DANDELION SEEDS

"Now we can go on without being under the control of the archdiocese, which we know can't be trusted. My whole life sitting in front of the person preaching from that altar, they told us that "this is your church"... That was absolutely untrue."

—*Parishioner at St. Frances X. Cabrini Parish in Scituate, MA*

While wholesale parish defection from a parish in a major diocese in response to an ecclesiastical directive commands a great deal of press, there are many other small, intentional Eucharistic communities that have grown up around the country in the last decade as a result of the church's treatment of women and gay people, the unresolved wounds of the sexual abuse scandal, and the high-handed behavior of the clergy. While the formation of these communities is not dramatic or their membership as large as Spiritus Christi, St. Stephen, St. Peter, St. Stanislaus, and St. Dominic, these small communities that exist across the nation are providing another model of church to Catholics tired of top-down, harmful, and ill-conceived hierarchical decisions. Many of these small communities are based upon variations of the Dutch Dominican model presented in the previous chapter. All are building the church of tomorrow in the midst of institutional failure.

Some of these intentional Eucharistic communities have hundreds of parishioners, for example Mary Magdalene Apostle Community in San Diego, California. Some have satellite sites to accommodate parishioners who live great distances away, as does the Community of Saint Mary Magdalene in Philadelphia. Many are quite small and meet in people's homes, just like Christians did in the early church. Almost all of the larger communities rent out space in friendly Protestant churches, synagogues, or in the community rooms of schools or nursing homes. (A list of Intentional Eucharistic Communities will appear in the appendix.)

For the most part, these communities are pastored by women priests and male, married priests, some affiliated with the Federation of Christian Ministries, the Old Catholic, or the Ecumenical Catholic Communion, or by women ordained by Roman Catholic Womenpriests or the Association of Roman Catholic Women Priests.

Most of the ordained priests and members of the new communities once belonged to traditional Catholic parishes. Catholics who felt that they were no longer fed in traditional parishes have found a home in new, vibrant communities that recognize the authority and equality of all people under a loving God. Many Catholics have found a warm, loving, and, most importantly, safe haven in these alternative communities where all are welcomed and fed without exception. In these communities, presiding and preaching become a ministry of responsibility rather than an exercise of power, exclusion, or fear.

This new way of being church does not require a bishop's permission. Rather than falling into a vortex over which they have no control, the People of God in these communities are free to solve their own problems. The only voices that can close down these parishes are the voices of the community members themselves. The bishop's authority, while respected, no longer affects the spirit, the charism, or the operation of the newly formed parishes.

To provide an example of what the Spirit makes possible, I will share with you a description of my own intentional Eucharistic community, which meets in a suburb of Philadelphia and in Palmyra, New Jersey.

Caryl Conroy Johnson and I are co-pastors of The Community of St. Mary Magdalene. St. Mary Magdalene formed after my ordination as a Roman Catholic woman priest in 2006. The community comprises congregants who for reasons mentioned at the beginning of the chapter could no longer worship in a traditional Roman Catholic parish. While respecting the traditions that provided the framework for both their religious experiences and spiritual lives, parish members felt that the Holy Spirit was leading them into something new and different and, for them, more life-giving. The community grew organically along those lines, holding fast to traditional worship while growing together into a liturgical style that respected the equality of all members of the Body of Christ.

As a result of this understanding, the parish adopted non-sexist language to refer to God. After the homily, the congregation has been empowered to reflect upon their interpretation of the Scriptures read at Mass. The parish relies upon the transformational power of God to guide the shape of their worship, which remains open to any seeker without any conditions attached. Everyone, regardless of their denomination or the state of his or her soul is always welcome to the communion table, courtesy of Jesus in whom, as Paul wrote so beautifully in Galatians 3:28, "There is no Jew nor Gentile, no slave nor free, there is no male nor female, for all are one in Christ Jesus."

The Community of St. Mary Magdalene rents a spacious chapel, graced with colorful stained-glass windows depicting the creation, in a United Methodist Church in a Philadelphia suburb for a nominal fee. The chapel is generally available for other services during the week, such as Ash Wednesday, Holy Thursday, or for Bible study or other activities. A dining room and a gym are also available for use when necessary. The church allows the use of the main sanctuary in the event of a funeral or a wedding. Because of the generosity and support of our United Methodist hosts, the Community of St. Mary Magdalene can provide its parishioners with all of the sacraments, as do traditional Catholic parishes, making it a church community in every respect.

The parish is financially self-sufficient. Because the space is rented and not owned, there is very little overhead aside from rents and small stipends for the musician and the priests. No time or money is spent on managing a large plant. There are also no worries about meeting financial deadlines or needing to have giving campaigns to raise money to keep the parish operating. Thus, the parish is able to give away a significant amount of money collected to charities such as Water for Kenya, Dawn's Place (a safe haven for formerly trafficked women), orphanages in Honduras, and homeless shelters, to name a few. The parish is incorporated into a nonprofit entity, so all giving is tax deductible. The pastors do not handle any money. A treasurer collects the money, keeps financial records, and makes monthly reports on finances. All financial decisions are made at well-attended monthly community meetings.

Since the parish is run as a discipleship of equals and espouses the common priesthood of all believers, all members of the community have an equal voice in running and maintaining the parish. The priest has no more power than any other member of the community. Committees spontaneously arose to care for the chapel space and to provide linens, bake bread, and purchase wine and flowers each week. The same is true of those serving as lectors, Eucharistic ministers, and hosts after Mass each Sunday.

No organization, however well meaning, is exempt from controversy. People who attend the Community of St. Mary Magdalene vary in their theological, social, and political opinions, as do those who attend traditional Catholic churches. Because everyone has a voice, all members of the community are invited and encouraged to express their opinions at monthly community meetings, where fellow congregants may or may not agree. Since the community adheres to the democratic process, all motions are put to a vote. The congregation does its very best to hold fast to the law of love while in the midst of sometimes painful disagreements.

The Community of St. Mary Magdalene began with a core group of ten people. Growth over the years has been slow but steady. On any given Sunday, between thirty and forty people gather together to worship God. There are approximately seventy people on the parish rolls. Another twelve meet for worship in a satellite community in nearby New Jersey. The relatively small size of the community enables a time of deep sharing after the homily and during the petitions, which would be impossible with a larger group.

It is important to remember that every intentional community will be different and will grow differently and will have different worship styles. However, several important truths emerge from the delicate task of community/church building in the new millennium. The most important element is, of course, the people, whoever they are, with whatever baggage that comes along with them. The Lutheran martyr Dietrich Bonhoeffer wrote that a parish consists of whomever God sends, not what the parish or the pastor seeks or wants. The second is love, the mortar that holds the process together and must prevail over every other concern and issue. The third is transparency. Within a parish community, there should be no secrets. An awareness of these three elements should mitigate the many surprises and challenges that are sure to test the community during the delicate time of formation. It is important to remember that all communities, while inspired by God, are of human construction and will make mistakes. Charity requires that all members bear with one another.

Starting up and maintaining a new community apart from an established institution with many resources requires hard work on the part of all community members since there is no overarching financial framework or personnel department to support it. However, the process of community building makes people strong, resilient, and knowledgeable about their faith.

Some might ask, Are the newly formed communities mentioned "really" Catholic, or are they something else? While this is a good question, the better adjective to use might be "authentic." Are the people authentically worshipping God? Are they authentically following the Gospel? Is God authentically present in their midst and in the Eucharist?

Authentic worship in an authentic community does not depend upon a group of human beings, however theologically well-trained, who think they control the Almighty and can orchestrate divine presence. All Christians know that God is everywhere. Jesus himself said that wherever two or more are gathered in His name, there He will be, so God is very much present in intentional Eucharistic communities.

Visitors to services in these hierarchically unsanctioned but authentic assemblies are often moved to tears, as I was when worshipping for the first time at Spiritus Christi, where God was palpably present in our midst. Grown men and women have unabashedly wept at the ordinations of women priests as the People of God moved forward into a new vision of church.

In addition, the apostle Paul bequeathed to us an excellent way of determining if the actions the People of God have taken are, indeed, authentically of God. Successful, God-inspired enterprises, including church building, produce the fruits of the Holy Spirit:

charity, joy, peace, patience, goodness, kindness, generosity, gentleness, and faithfulness. As Jesus famously said, "By their fruits, you shall know them."[1] These fruits tend to become sour and prickly in the presence of hard-heartedness inspired by absolute power coupled with mandatory obedience.

A prime example of this bitter fruit is Philadelphia Archbishop Chaput's October 2016 address at Notre Dame University, where he essentially used the uncharitable and ill-conceived practice of showing the door to those who disagree with ecclesiastical actions. For Chaput and some of his bishop brothers, a diminished church minus discontents is preferable to those who welcome and include everyone, including those Jesus as the Good Shepherd would have actively pursued as they floundered along the byways of lives often gone wrong. Chaput labels those who do not follow his edicts as "cowards" who "perpetrate violence against those who do believe and do seek to live according to God's word," again confusing human words with the Word of God, which directs that all of us, including bishops, love our neighbor as ourselves, forgiving seventy times seven.[2] There are no expressions of charity, kindness, or generosity in these sentiments.

Few would deny that practicing one's faith by following God's directive to love our neighbor as ourselves is difficult. The exercise of conscience and faithfulness to Jesus' kingdom message is often accompanied by sacrifice and sometimes life-altering or threatening consequences. However, church should not be this mean and hard-hearted.

This scorched-earth pastoral policy highlights the difference between authenticity and authority. An authentic Christian follows Christ by adhering to the two great commandments taught by Jesus to love God and all that God loves, and Christians know that God loves everyone without judgmental human caveats. Upon these two commandments, Jesus said, the entire law rests. It is, then, the practice of the cardinal virtue of love that gives authority to religious leaders in any and all sects to teach and preach about God and to lead congregations. The authoritative command from church leaders to believe, to obey, and to follow without question does not necessarily give rise to love, which ultimately is the only force that can transform the self and, by extension, the world. The insistent and myopic focus upon obedience also belittles divine power and renders God a petty idol who must use violence to ensure belief.

An insistence upon obedience also tends to divide Catholics into opposing camps with carefully drawn lines. In these sectarian camps, charity and love cannot prevail. God gets crowded out in a place lacking love. The reality is that an effortlessly recited creed, frequent praying of the rosary, and a flawlessly executed Mass can remain hopelessly un-Christian if unaccompanied by love.

Benedictine Sister Joan Chittister has frequently commented in her many books on the yawning gap between the beliefs and the practice of the Christian faith and the way the world looks. And so authority, perhaps based upon great faith strong enough to move mountains, when unaccompanied by love that endures all things, hopes all things, and forgives all things is nothing but sounding brass. The Apostle Paul wrote that faith and, by extension, leadership is, in the end, inauthentic without love. Unloving and uncharitable leadership often leads to hypocrisy, both by leaders and by the flock.

Pope Francis discussed the difference between our faith and the state of the world in a homily in February 2017:

> But what is scandal? Scandal is saying one thing and doing another; it is a double life, a double life. A totally double life: "I am very Catholic, I always go to Mass, I belong to this association and that one; but my life is not Christian, I don't pay my workers a just wage, I exploit people, I am dirty in my business, I launder money... " A double life. And so many Christians are like this, and these people scandalize others. How many times have we heard—all of us, around the neighborhood and

elsewhere—"But to be a Catholic like that, it's better to be an atheist." It is that, scandal. You destroy. You beat down. And this happens every day, it's enough to see the news on TV, or to read the papers. In the papers there are so many scandals, and there is also the great publicity of the scandals. And with the scandals there is destruction.

The very idea of a small, mean, lean church is a scandal to God. Such words are an affront to the power and majesty of our big-hearted, all-loving God who sends divine love pressed down and overflowing into everyone's laps.

Since God is love writ large, the proliferation of new and varied religious communities is something that the divine would desire rather than condemn. God does not require or condone a human-defined unity. The centuries are filled with people who formed different groups devoted to worshipping God in different ways. Every iteration—if it produced the gifts of the Spirit—fleshed out rather than diminished the presence of the divine, enlarging the Body of Christ. When left unmolested and unjudged, all worked for the greater glory of God and humanity. So will any new intentional Eucharistic community, however it hovers on the edge of the pale.

Ultimately, the happy reality of the Christian faith is that what seems to separate one Christian group from another is so insignificant it is really not worth mentioning. While our ancestors in faith bequeathed to us what seems to be intractable sectarian dissention that excluded and persecuted the "other," we know from Scripture that all Christians profess one faith, one Lord, and one baptism. All Christians read the same Scripture and acknowledge it as the Word of God. All profess the same creed. This impressive similarity that is beautifully expressed in Ephesians 4:5 is the reason most Protestant denominations now welcome other Christians to the communion table, a table that belongs to God rather than to a priest or a bishop, a table where all are fed and welcomed, just the way they are.

Open table fellowship reflects Jesus' vision of the great banquet where people from all over the world come and sit together, sharing their food and, in the process of eating a meal, their lives. When people eat together as friends at a common table, a vast door opens up to expose the panoply of authentic human experiences that join all of us as family rather than as foes. From this sharing, transformation can proceed. From table fellowship, true unity is born. Uniformity, which requires authority to enforce, is, of course, something completely different.

CHAPTER SEVEN
TECTONICS

"When the history and cultural context shifts,
guess what's right behind it? The expression
of religious life shifts to match it."

—*Carol Zinn, SSJ*

For those who wonder if small church communities are a viable way of worshipping God, it must be remembered that small faith communities have an historical precedent. The early Christians continued to observe the Sabbath on Saturdays in the temple after the death and resurrection of Jesus, per Acts of the Apostles. They also met in house churches, shared a common meal to remember Jesus, and read from whatever holy book they might have had since the New Testament would not exist for another three hundred years or so.[1] Contrary to Scripture, which often lists "thousands" of converts at its beginning, Christianity was a very small affair that did not separate completely from Judaism until the late first century. Like the people of today, it took time and prayer for people to leave the comfort of their respective faiths and become Christians, a move which often placed them in conflict with their families, their friends, and the religious authorities. Christianity did not become large enough to have buildings regarded as churches until it became the state religion of the Roman Empire. Until then, the early Christians worshipped in house churches presided over by the owners of the house, who were both women and men.

We hear of these early house churches in Paul's letter to the Romans, which was written twenty or more years before any of the gospels. In Romans, chapter 16, Paul addresses greetings to the movers and shakers of the early church in Rome, recommending Phoebe, the leader of the church at Cenchreae, and Prisca and Aquila, whose house church had been the church in Rome in the early 50s CE before being expelled, along with the Jews they resembled, from Rome by the Emperor Claudius. Paul lists men and many women and describes them as "working hard in the Lord"; that is, they were leaders in their church community. Interestingly enough, the name of Peter, the later symbol of church power in Rome, is not among them. Other members of the "twelve" are also conspicuously absent from Paul's list.

Paul's other letters indicate that many of the early church leaders were women. Aside from Prisca, Paul mentions Mary, Junia (the prominent apostle), Tryphosa, the "beloved" Persis, and Julia.[2] Paul apparently worked closely with these women, and they were important enough for him to mention them by name, some with titles of authority. Leaders in the early church rose organically from the assembly of the people. Their gender didn't matter since all had been made one in Jesus Christ.[3]

Ordination in the modern sense did not exist, and the only priest Jesus, Paul, and the early converts in Palestine would have known would have been the high priest in Jerusalem. Jesus never used the words *priest* and *ordination*, and neither did Paul. Instead, Paul used the word *diakonos* or deacon. He uses that same word to refer to Phoebe, the female leader of the church at Cenchreae.

The Greek word *diakonos* means servant or waiter and is hardly an honorific term indicating any kind of prestige.

The egalitarian nature of the nascent church unfortunately only lasted until the end of the first century, as Christianity adapted to the cultural mores of the time, which did not encourage or respect the equality of the sexes. As in Sister Carol Zinn's comment at the beginning of this chapter, religious life makes the shift along with culture and society, even when it takes steps away from the good news of the gospel and fails to produce the fruits of the Spirit. None of the people mentioned above, including both Paul and Peter, could have imagined what the Way of Jesus would become in a couple of centuries.

When Christians did begin to build churches after aligning with the Roman Empire, churches did not immediately become sacred edifices, holy in themselves. In his book *The Early Liturgy to the Time of Gregory the Great*, Josef Jungmann wrote that early Christian churches were built as an honored place for the assembled community to meet once they grew too large to meet in people's homes. However, the actual walls, the icons, and even the clergy were secondary to the sense of the community that met to worship God in spirit and in truth.[4] In fact, the earliest name of the church was "house of the assembly." Only later did the building where the community came to meet become known as church, eventually acquiring other connotations. In the beginning, it was the People of God that held pride of place.

Travelers to Europe have seen the very ancient, very tiny, very primitive churches that are scattered across the countryside. Throughout history, churches located in the small villages and towns throughout Europe were this small with the big cathedrals reserved for major cities like Paris, Cologne, and Rome. Small church communities were the rule in the early days of America as well, until the major cities grew due to the large influx of Catholic immigrants in the late nineteenth and early twentieth centuries. This huge growth in the Catholic population necessitated the building of the large urban parishes—the very ones that are now on the decline.

Thus, Catholics in America have become accustomed to worshipping in large fancy churches with stained-glass windows, marble columns, statues, and ornate, gold-trimmed ceilings, all of which were paid for by the original members of the parish, who gave what was in many cases their meager dollars to build their parish church. Many people still prefer to worship in these big fancy churches because church doesn't seem like church without a sizeable building and a clergy attired in expensive ceremonial dress, in spite of Christianity's humble beginnings.

However, meaningful worship occurs just as well in small churches, in chapels, and in the home, as those who once attended home Masses know so well. Consequently, there is no need for church to be a big, fancy affair with a big overhead. Church is, and always has been, the People of God gathered together in the holy name of Jesus. Consequently, what we call church functions as well in a rented space or in a family living room as it does in a grand cathedral with incense and a bishop's throne, just as it did in a village church designed for twenty people so many years ago.

Theologian John Dick expresses the worth of small faith communities in his blog, *Another Voice*:

> Yes! We need to put on our thinking caps, because we need to shift from large congregations to intimate small size communities. Large parishes can be divided into smaller neighborhood prayer groups and study groups. Mega churches have the energy of a football game; but small communities have the energy of the human heart. This is not downsizing but reconfiguring.[5]

Just as church buildings have changed over the centuries, so has the church, in spite of protestations to the contrary. Catholics might have forgotten or not know how much church teaching and practice, which did not emerge fully formed from the acts and ideas of the apostles in the first century CE, have changed over the course of the last two millennia.

In the beginning, for example, the Jesus movement was a literal hodgepodge of different Christianities splashed across southeastern Europe, North Africa, and the Middle East. The tenets of these groups—the Nestorians, the Ebionites, the Apollinarians, the Pelagians, the Sabellians, and the Arians, just to name a few—developed at the beginning of Christianity as followers of Jesus tried to figure out how to be Christian. Each worshipped in a different manner, read from their particular sacred books, and developed their own theologies, which contained their own nugget of truth that led them to God.

It took a couple of church councils called by Roman emperors and almost five hundred years to determine that Jesus was consubstantial with the Father and had both a human and divine nature. It took about the same amount of time for the twenty-seven books of the Christian Bible to be canonized into what Christians call the New Testament from among the scores of sacred books that had been written in the course of those four hundred years. What became the prayers and liturgical practices of the Mass were determined by political as well as religious powers. It was not until the eleventh century that the pope had the power to demand the standardization the liturgy.

This variation in teaching and practice continued in the Middle Ages. In the early days of Christian worship, the people were active participants in the Mass who responded aloud to prayers said by the bishop or the presiding priest. By the eleventh century, the custom changed as the liturgy became the sole province of the ordained priest rather than "the work of the people." The priest now whispered the liturgical prayers at an altar placed against the back wall of the church, away from the eyes and ears of the assembly. In some churches huge rood screens divided the priest and the Eucharist from the people of God. No longer able to see or hear what was transpiring on the altar, the people began to engage in private devotional practices during Mass that had nothing to do with the liturgy.

It was not until the Council of Trent (1545–1563) that the Church systematized liturgical practices, reduced the number of sacraments to seven, defined transubstantiation, and reformed the many abuses that led to the Reformation. It wasn't until Vatican II that the people regained their voice during the liturgy.

As this little snippet of church history demonstrates, change is always assured. Nature itself teaches us that the only thing that is certain about life is that things will change. Glaciers grow and make their way to the sea and then melt. Great mountain chains form huge peaks and then wear down through erosion. Volcanoes erupt, burying once vibrant towns. Ice ages come and go. Great groups of people migrate from one place to another due to changes in weather patterns, natural disaster, famine, or war. New religions grow and overpower the old. Great civilizations fade away. Nothing is guaranteed forever, and eternity is a long time for things to remain the status quo.

As Stephen Cox suggests in his 2014 book *American Christianity*, nothing and nobody can really prevent change from happening. The New Testament, with its perennial call to conversion and transformation, serves as a "provocation for change." Even the most hierarchical denominations are not, Cox writes, immune to change from both within and without and from both the bottom and the top.

> It is impossible to find an American religious group that turns the same face to the world today that it did one hundred or even fifty years ago. Instead of staying in one place, American churches have wandered across the landscape, abandoning old sources of support and discovering new ones, in a continual process of self-conversion.[6]

The proliferation of huge Pentecostal and non-denominational churches both in the United States and in once solidly Catholic South America, coupled with the diminishment of once-prominent mainstream Protestant denominations, prove Cox's point.

In addition, all Christian denominations, including Catholicism, are exposed to what Cox calls "the DNA of the New Testament," which leads followers of Jesus to discover new meanings in ancient words, actions, and rites.

An example of this is the development and evolution of Catholic sacramental theology. Catholics have been taught that Jesus instituted the seven sacraments during his short life and that these sacraments have remained unchanged for two thousand years. Joseph Martos is one of many theologians who has written that this understanding of the sacraments is simply untrue. In his book *Deconstructing Sacramental Theology and Reconstructing Catholic Ritual*, Martos asserts that the church arrived at this fairly recent understanding of the sacraments by uncritically interpreting ancient texts from the earliest days of Christianity and then passing mistaken ideas onto succeeding generations of people. Instead, Martos argues, the nature of the sacraments evolved, along with doctrine and practice, as the church was exposed to different cultures and ideas throughout the ages.[7]

In addition, the Roman Catholic Church is, of course, as much a social and political entity as it is a religious one. Knee deep in whatever culture in which it has existed, the church has always adapted to the prevailing social and political environment. As mentioned earlier in the book, the faith of a poor man dedicated to the care of the poor morphed into an imperial cult with a supreme ruler and a court of princes once it moved out of people's homes and into the emperor's palace. Consequently, what appears to be a current radical shift of moving towards small Eucharistic communities guided by members of the community rather than by an organized hierarchy might not seem to be so radical at all in light of the many changes that have occurred across two millennia.

Armed with the New Testament motif of change and transformation, parishioners should feel empowered to resurrect what appears to be their dead parish. As scriptural stories of the Resurrection teach us so well, the reality of new life may look somewhat different from what we are used to seeing or believing. In the beginning, for instance, none of the disciples—including Mary Magdalene, who is described in the Gospel of Philip as "one of the three who always walked with the Lord"—recognized Jesus after his resurrection. Only with further reflection and prayer do we, like Mary and the rest of the disciples, understand that the new form of life that we see approaching is, indeed, a new manifestation of the old.

In these early years of the twenty-first century, we are fortunate to live in a time of seismic change. Who would have thought in the 1930s that African American people would be finally granted civil rights, imperfect as those rights appear to be as currently applied? Who would have thought in the 1970s or -80s that gay people would eventually be given the right to marry in 2015 or that an African American man could become the president of the United States?

Likewise, who in the 1960s would have ever thought that the mighty churches that soared above communities all over America and Europe would be closing a mere fifty years later? Who would have ever thought that a pope might even suggest that his fellow Catholics should refrain from judging others? Who would have imagined that people would just get tired of clerical prejudices and power and just go ahead and ordain women in spite of the fact that John Paul II directed Catholics not to even think about women's ordination?

Who could even imagine that we would be in the place we are today where all sorts of seemingly permanent and irreformable ideas about humanity and religious faith are cracking and changing and moving and melting like huge glaciers subjected to global warming?

At this point in time, we really have no idea where we, as a church, are all going. The church is like a glacier calving and losing a huge part of itself on the way to becoming something else, and there seems to be little anyone can do to stop what is obviously becoming inevitable. The future, as always, is secured by visionaries.

Just as the Protestant Reformation proved to be the end of Roman Catholic hegemony in the western world five hundred years ago, the current numbers crisis indicate that something very new is afoot in the world of religion. The internet has made all information both good and bad instantaneously available to those in the western world. There can be no hiding of scandal, no cover-up of misdeeds, no explaining away the great wealth of a church crying poor, and no masking of the chronic misogyny and homophobia that hobbles what could be a great church. Thus, there will be no return to the age of faith that many imagined to have existed in a golden past.

Sister of St. Joseph Carol Zinn aptly expressed the change that is enveloping the Catholic Church as religious orders and the clergy continue their downward spiral into what Zinn believes will be actual oblivion. In her address at the Resource Center for Religious Institutes in October of 2016, Zinn warned of the end of religious life in North America, Europe, and Australia because of the huge social and cultural shifts that have occurred in the last hundred years. Regrouping, selling off property, and curtailing mission, she said, are just sustaining the present unsustainable model, a model that has no future. Rather than bemoaning its end and hoping for a return to veils and habits and obedient women as a way of boosting membership in religious life, Zinn rejoiced in the fact that God always makes all things new saying, "There's joy that God is in charge. It will go as God wants it to go."[8]

Thus, the church has changed in the past. The church will change in the present. The church will change in the future.

What has been called "the barque of Peter" is sailing again into a sea of the unknown that stretches before Catholics with vast possibilities placed there by God, who sends Her breath regularly across the face of the deep to cleanse and purify it. The hierarchy can continue to constrain a living faith by continuing to smother it with the encrustations of an ancient, pagan philosophical system of immutable forms, or it can expand its heart and mind and soul to include the myriad modern ideas that are pointing in a different direction. Those ideas that don't come from God will eventually fall away without fulminations or excommunications from the top, just as Rabbi Gamaliel promised in Acts 5:34.

The stage has been set for the assortment and growth of churches that we see today. This array should not be perceived as disunity or a fracturing from an ideal, but rather as a new way for people to raise their voices and praise God. These voices all sing of one Lord, one faith, one creed, and one baptism. If these churches follow Jesus' command to love one another and produce the fruits of the Holy Spirit, then that church is the church of Jesus Christ. Those who are able to make this great leap of faith will sing this new church, a church gathered in the name of Jesus that trusts the goodness of creation and is marked by holiness and light, into being.[9]

The good news is that God is always in the process of creating a new heavens and a new earth—and a new church—from the unacknowledged and unredeemed mistakes of the past. Not to recognize or prevent this change is to set sin in stone. God has chosen the People of God to move the church into a new century, with its bright future. It behooves them to catch the great ball of possibilities that God has thrown to them.

Chapter Eight
The Adult Dance

"What we can do is to delegitimate an unjust system and create a spiritual counter climate."

—*Walter Wink*

For those of you reading this, the end of your parish is either in sight or is becoming a distinct possibility. Some of you may have seen it coming. Perhaps your numbers were down. Maybe old parishioners had died off and young people seem uninterested. Perhaps the physical plant was too old and too expensive to maintain. Others, like the members or parishes mentioned in previous chapters, might have full coffers, pews filled to capacity, and extensive programming but not enough celibate male priests.

For some, the news about your parish closing might have been whispered down the lane, neighbor to neighbor, as things often happen in local communities. Some might have read it in the newspaper; others will hear it on the television. Sometimes the pastor is forced to announce the bad news from the pulpit with little or no warning.

As discussed earlier in the book, these announcements are not accompanied by kindness, gentleness, tact, or charity. Father Joseph Mecir, former pastor of Sacred Heart of Jesus in Cleveland, expressed both his surprise and his confusion when he learned that his parish was slated to close.

> This is a real blow to us. We were not expecting this at all. We are the only parish in Slavic Village [in Cleveland] whose bills are paid. We are not in the red at all. We have no idea why this came about.[1]

In his book Render Unto Rome, Jason Berry reported that in 2007 Cardinal Edward Egan of New York summoned the pastor of an ethnic parish in Manhattan into his office and told the poor guy that his parish was being closed and padlocked as they spoke![2]

Or, perhaps, you might be anxiously awaiting an answer from your appeal to Rome, like St. Laurentius Parish in Philadelphia did, spending over a hundred thousand dollars in legal fees, only to be shut out of discussions made in secret about their twinned parish and castigated by the archbishop for working to designate their church as historical in a last-ditch effort to keep it from being demolished. Or, like St. Frances Xavier Cabrini in Scituate, Massachusetts, you might have occupied your parish building for twelve years, finally taking your case to keep your parish open all the way to the Supreme Court.

Or perhaps your bishop announced the closing one Sunday and then locked the door behind you on the way out. Whether your bishop declares your parish dead via parish announcement or in the newspaper or from the pulpit, your feelings will likely be the same. You may feel stunned, dismayed, disrespected, upset, hurt, and angry.

What should you and parishioners like you do?

First of all, never take "no" for the final answer. As I have written repeatedly, Father really doesn't know best. Be assured that there are ways to keep your parish alive in spite of the episcopal "no." Keep the examples of Spiritus Christi in Rochester, St. Peter in Cleveland, St. Stanislaus in St. Louis, and St. Stephen in Minneapolis close to your heart. Refuse to capitulate to unjust power. Do not choose to remain faithful under structures of domination. While you might be operating in unexplored territory, never fear, for God will be with you.

There are, however, some practical considerations you need to keep before you. As a resurrection people, Catholics understand that rising from the dead entails transformation, renewal, and change. Therefore, know that a parish that rises from the ashes of the old may not look or feel exactly like the parish of origin. In fact, it may seem very different at first glance. As mentioned previously, the resurrected Jesus looked so different from his regular self that none of his closest companions recognized him. After his death, the fledgling community that had grown up around him had to reorganize itself to reflect his physical absence. The reorganization looked very different from what the disciples had come to regard as usual. Like the early church communities that developed after the death of Jesus, your new community will, however it eventually comes together, remain your parish, even though it will now exist in a new, resurrected form.

Because your parish has been resurrected, feel free to retain the name of your beloved parish even as you meet in a different venue, just as communities like Spiritus Christi, St. Peter, and St. Stephen did. Remember your parish will be what you make it to be—just as it always has been.

One of the first steps in keeping your parish alive is to gather people together who do not wish to see their parish community dissolve, always keeping in mind that the parish belongs to the People of God, rather than to the bishop. Discern within that core group if there is enough will and energy to carry out this goal. It is important to remember that a core group of ten can grow over time, just as the early church did. In addition, every person in the parish does not need to sign on in order to form the new entity. A resurrected parish can function quite well with a small group of determined people.

Look for guidance from established small faith communities and house churches in your area, if there are any in existence. A listing of many intentional Eucharistic communities can be found at www.intentionaleucharistic.org. The Federation of Christian Ministries (FCM), CORPUS, Roman Catholic Womenpriests (RCWP), and the Association of Roman Catholic Women Priests (ARCWP) have ordained priests who can either serve as mentors to you as you plan your resurrected parish or as the presiders in your new, resurrected parish community. Keep in mind that early communities were headed by women and that most of the apostles, including Peter, were married men.

Liturgical resources such as new and used sacramentaries and lectionaries can be purchased online. The Quixote Center sells an inclusive lectionary containing the readings for Mass for years A, B, and C online. Some intentional communities have decided to use biblical readings other than those in the lectionary, which omits verses devoted to the actions of powerful women, such as the brave midwives Shiprah and Puah (in Exodus), Huldah (the prophet in 2 Chronicles 34:22), Phoebe (the deacon), and Junia (the apostle mentioned in Romans 16).

Many of the communities that have been mentioned have used Eucharistic prayers and other prayers that do not contain the unwieldy, male-centered, archaic language of the new sacramentary and are, thus, more user friendly. Those liturgical resources can be made available by the groups mentioned above.

Since Jesus probably offered a cup roughly hewn out of wood to his friends at the Last Supper rather a chalice or a plate of gold or silver, resurrected communities should feel free to use wine cups, decorative plates, and dinner napkins for use during the celebration of the Eucharist. The Last Supper was a family Seder celebration rather than a feast for royalty, so things common to the home rather than to the palace of a king were used. It is not necessary to purchase expensive precious metal cups and plates and linens. Jesus is Emmanuel, God with us as one of us. A poor tradesman who lived among and served the poorest of the poor, Jesus would not feel honored by the use of gold or silver place settings or expensive linens.

It is important for the discerning group to determine when, where, and how often your newly resurrected parish will meet. The experience of existing small faith communities indicates that communities should meet every Sunday. Otherwise, people will either not attend Mass on a regular basis, forget the date, or find another place to worship. Be aware that communities, like flowers, need time to grow, so do not worry if your community begins small and remains that way for some time. Have faith in the workings of the Spirit. The house churches of the early Christian movement prove that size is immaterial.

Your resurrected community could meet in the homes of different parishioners each week, or in rented space in a Protestant church, or in a meeting room in a nursing home or a school. Many Protestant churches and synagogues rent out spaces for a small fee.

Or course, if you rent space in a church or in a meeting room, you will need to find the funds with which to pay your host church. You will also need funds to purchase wine and the ingredients to make bread, to purchase the lectionary and sacramentary, and any other items you might need. You can also use hosts which can be ordered online or purchased at religious stores. The parishioners will, then, need to continue to tithe in order to pay the bills. It will then be necessary to form a nonprofit corporation, a 501(c)3 organization. The IRS recognizes any church as tax exempt, but in the long run, the nonprofit status, which is neither difficult nor burdensome to obtain, is ultimately desirable.

Healthy communities can survive only through open dialogue and shared experiences. If resurrected parishes hope to grow, they should not ever employ the "power tools" used by their bishops. As poet Audre Lorde wrote, "The master's tools will never dismantle the master's house."

It is important that all members have a voice in community building, even when there is disagreement and things sometimes get unpleasant. Democracy is a messy, imperfect, and time-consuming process. However, pulling rank and making unilateral decisions is a recipe for disaster. So is the development of cliques. Transparency in all things is, therefore, an absolute necessity. Consequently, all decisions should be made by the community rather than by either the presider or any type of leadership committee. If all voices are not heard, resentment builds and your new parish will fall apart. The beauty of small communities is that all voices can be easily heard.

It is vitally important for new parishes to have monthly meetings where parishioners can discuss and vote upon parish business and practices. It is not recommended that the liturgical leader run these meetings. Nor is it recommended that the liturgical leader manage the finances. Instead, a finance committee should handle the money. Ensuring transparency with finances is one of the most important steps a new community can make as it forms.

Experience with small faith groups has indicated that in most cases, parishioners gravitate towards the area where they are most skilled or most comfortable. Thus some members might elect to care for the environment of the worship area. Others become readers or Eucharistic ministers. Some bake the bread. Others might have the experience to care for the parish finances. Another might become the music minister. Some members are called to preach. It is important that from the beginning all the work of the parish should not fall upon the shoulders of just a few people as this will lead to burnout. The beauty of the resurrected community is that it belongs to everyone. Thus, everyone has a role in maintaining it.

Some parishioners might feel the need for a bishop to administer the sacrament of confirmation. Both Roman Catholic Womenpriests and the Association of Roman Catholic Women Priests (RCWP, ARCWP) have bishops who can be called upon to administer the sacraments of confirmation and holy orders. These bishops live in areas across the United States, in some parts of Canada, in Colombia, South America, and in Germany and Austria. The bishops in North America were elected by the priests in their areas. Unlike the male bishops in the institutional church, the women bishops in RCWP and ARCWP do not demand obedience from either priests or parishioners. They do not oversee worship practices or interfere in the workings of the intentional parish and serve rather as consultants and pastors to the pastors. The bishops—like the priests—follow a different model of priesthood where the ordained promise to follow the Gospel rather than a human being. Of course, worshipping God does not require a permit in the United States, and experience indicates that bishops do not necessarily ensure unity.

As people reconcile themselves to the reality that the number of ordained, male priests will continue to drop drastically over the upcoming decades, resulting in ongoing and massive church closings, it is important to know that the concept of priesthood and the understanding of ordination have changed over the millennia.

The earliest understanding of priesthood included the belief that a priest was ordained to a specific parish for a certain amount of time. Their ordination was reserved to that place. Once the priest left that place, he or she reverted to his or her original place among the faithful. There was no understanding of an ontological change or an infusion of sanctity that brought certain privileges, and thus, there was no need for laicization. When the term of service as priest in the community ended, the community chose another person to serve as priest. This ancient practice of priesthood, which empowers the People of God to choose their own leaders, could be an antidote for the priest shortage. As in the past, this position would remain open to all qualified members of the community, which in the modern world includes males as well as females, along with married, single, and gay people. The priest would serve at the pleasure of the community, just as they do in Protestant churches.

Of course, the journey to resurrecting your parish will not be easy or problem-free. It will necessitate hard work, dedication, and study, as well as open hearts and open minds. Do not, as expressed in 1 Timothy 4:14, neglect the gift that is in you. Never give up hope.

Chapter Nine
Upside Down

"The exodus begins. Come, let us go."

—*Richard Marrone, pastor*
of the Community of St. Peter

T he prologue of this book began with a description of the
founding of the Community of the Christian Spirit in the
late 1960s. Almost fifty years ago, the Medical Missionary Sisters
who began the community dreamed the dreams described by the
prophet Joel. They, as well as the priests who led the services, were
prophets of what they believed would be a new movement in the
church. As the architects of CCS, they provided many opportunities
for innovative liturgies and lay participation. Their intention was
that the attendees would take these practices back to their staid and
sober local parishes and transform them as they and their parishioners had been transformed.

This was not to happen. While priests and pastors of the time
generally followed the guidelines put forth by Vatican II to update
the liturgy, pray in English, and turn the altar around so that the

priest faced the people, vibrant, outside-the-box liturgies were something many priests could not or would not do. The power, might, and conservatism of the local archbishop loomed over the parish priest, suppressing the very innovations that might have served as the magical evangelization tool for which the church would seek in vain for the next fifty years.

I attended one of these liturgies as a young college student. I recall the excitement, the joy, and the faith of the people who came to Mass because they wanted to, not because they had to under pain of mortal sin, the traditional belief at the time. My home parish served up lackluster liturgies each week presided over by too many priests, who behaved as if the new rite were a big mistake in which they were forced to participate under duress, rather than with joy. Homilies focused upon personal rather than structural sin even as the Vietnam War raged and young men from our parish were drafted into a war some of them did not support and white people were burning down the houses of black people in neighborhoods right next to ours. Because of the disconnect between life and liturgy, I rarely attended Mass in my home parish. It took me another fifteen years to find a parish that equaled the excitement and joy I felt at CCS.

In 1972, Cardinal Krol of Philadelphia, a prelate so conservative that he would not permit Saturday evening masses in spite of Pope Paul VI's permission to do so, sent the chancellor of the archdiocese to the Community of the Christian Spirit and directed all of the attendees to return to their parishes of origin. Rather than chance the very real threat of ecclesiastical sanctions against the sisters if the group continued to meet against the expressed wishes of the cardinal, the group began meeting elsewhere for worship with fewer attendees.

With the election of Pope John Paul II in 1978, liturgical experimentation came to a screeching halt. The reform of the reform began, and the stage was now set for a return to the clerical conservatism of the past. Over the course of his long reign, John Paul II, along with the like-minded bishops he appointed, walked back what they considered to be liturgical innovations. They insisted upon restoring archaic prayer forms that matched neither the patterns of modern speech nor modern thought. Sacramental rubrics needed to be followed scrupulously lest the sacrament "not take." Liturgical prayer reflected and enhanced male power. They tried mightily to restore the prestige of the priesthood to reflect a time when the priest ran the liturgical show, while parishioners prayed quietly and obediently in their pews, taking each clerical word as law and the voice of God. In returning to what the hierarchy believed to be an age of faith, the pope and the bishops sought to restore something that worked very well in a past where obedience to the clergy was imposed from above under threat of serious sin.

Conservative seminaries began producing restorationist priests dedicated to John Paul II. These priests often reintroduced traditionalist practices like the Gregorian Chant and Latin Masses, while homilies focused upon personal sin, abortion, and birth control rather than upon the good news that God loves us. These young priests, many of whom were prone to wearing cassocks and collars, also asserted what they believed was priestly authority over the non-ordained. Their high-handed treatment of parishioners led to complaints to the local bishop who, for the most part, ignored the parishioners and supported the priests.[1] Orthodox orders such as Opus Dei and the Legionaries of Christ also advanced the restorationist program. As a result of the emphasis upon obedience and authority, talk about women's ordination became verboten. Gay people became targets of diocesan witch hunts.

However, the reform rollback did not work as expected. The world had become a different place in spite of the Catholic hierarchy. This new world expected the bishops to listen to it as part of a respectful dialogue between equals. When this didn't happen, many people walked away from church.

So what kind of church do the bishops want in this new world? What kind of church do the parishioners want? It all depends upon the kind of God in which each group chooses to believe.

The kind of God we believe in directs our prayer life, our behavior, the organization of our parish communities, the governance of the church at large, our place in the world and in the church, as well as our worship style. If God is regarded as a supreme ruler who demands absolute obedience and issues membership guidelines, then the church is ruled by spiritual—and sometimes physical—violence as if God were not strong or mighty enough to attract love and service without human enforcement. That type of god requires a wealthy court of advisors dressed in fancy robes that expects their faithful followers to spy upon their sisters and brothers in Christ who appear not to toe the company line so any doctrinal contamination can be instantaneously eliminated.

Before Corpus Christi in Rochester became Spiritus Christi for instance, a man videoed the service each Sunday and sent a tape to the bishop. Trolls regularly comb the internet for evidence of alleged doctrinal infractions like homosexuality and report the information back to their bishop, who then summarily fires the dissenters from their jobs. Fear of the hierarchy is so strong that some pastors act preemptively and sack longtime parishioners just in the event their bishop finds out about alleged infractions. Beloved teachers and longtime parishioners lose their jobs for marrying their same sex spouses.

I was contacted by a member of my former beloved parish who was deputized by the pastor to tell me not to come to communion after the Vatican issued a statement stating that ordained women had automatically excommunicated themselves, just like women used to "get themselves pregnant" without benefit of man. The pastor, a good man overcome by fear of a vindictive bishop, had directed the Eucharistic ministers not to give me communion, even though I no longer attended the parish.

The court of bishops also conducted an inquisition of religious sisters. It has maligned books written by clergy or religious sisters like Margaret Farley and Elizabeth Johnson that offered theological viewpoints different from that of the hierarchy. It excommunicated an elderly theologian, Sri Lankan priest Tissa Balasuriya, for trying to portray Mary, the mother of Jesus, in a manner that made sense to the poor in Asia. In all of these cases, there were no trials and no discussions with any of the people involved, just decrees to repent or face the ecclesiastical music. Charity was conspicuously absent in each and every circumstance. Theologians who tried to contextualize God in a modern world were labeled as "a curse and affliction upon the church."[2]

The bishops' image of god requires big, fancy churches and gold vessels befitting a king. Only the self-selected clergy can touch anything pertaining to the sacred. These men, who reflect the male god they created, are mouthpieces for this god's words. In this model, things never can change because their god intended the world to be this way from the beginning. The past, which was never perfect and really did not exist in the way they imagine it, becomes an idol that distracts both the hierarchy and their flocks from following the two great commandments to love one another. In spite of the kinder, gentler faith seemingly espoused by Francis, fear rather than love remains the guiding principle of the Catholic Church.

On the other hand, the life of Jesus, our Emmanuel, God with us as one of us, provides us with a very different image. Jesus, the reason for the Christian faith, believed in a big-hearted, all-loving God whom he called "Father" or "Daddy" rather than Lord or Master. Following the example of his "Daddy" God, Jesus loved people so much that he fed them, cured them, cried over them, and even raised them from the dead, without ever once asking or caring if they deserved it. He ate with all sorts of unsavory characters and never asked for a person's life history before he helped them. He also lived life to the fullest, dining out with Zacchaeus and Martha and Mary. His detractors regarded him as a lush.

Jesus never berated anyone for sin—except for the religious authorities and the wealthy, whom he considered hypocrites. All who followed Jesus' command to care for the poor and the sick and the suffering were welcome into the Kingdom of God, the message he preached during his public life, the ideal for which he gave his life.

The God of Jesus actively sought for the lost sheep rather than shutting the gate and leaving him or her out of the fold. Jesus taught his followers that the Spirit of God, so obviously present in him, was poured out on all of them as well in equal measure. All they had to do was take advantage of what God gives to all people freely, pressed down and overflowing into their laps. As a result of Jesus' teaching and personal example, poor, fickle, fisher folk like Peter and Andrew, and women like Martha and Mary, felt the sacred power within them and went on to become leaders in the fledgling community. All of the early followers were less chosen than they were empowered by the Holy Spirit to preach the good news that God loved everyone beyond measure.

Acts of the Apostles tries to describe this empowerment in a speech attributed to Peter:

> I will pour out my Spirit on all humanity; your sons and your daughters will become prophets, your young men will see visions, and your old men dream dreams; yes, even on the slaves—for they are mine—both men and women, I will in those days pour out my Spirit.[3]

Empowering the people rather than reserving power for an elite group to do God's work can be messy. Some might view messiness as being somehow less than sacred. However, as Michael Morwood wrote, "Wherever the presence of God is one would expect to find variety, spontaneity, change, growth, development, new possibilities, adaptability, and even disorder."[4] Those acquainted with the power of this mighty Spirit know that She is neither neat nor orderly, but rather the energy and power of creation that belted out the universe in one unending cry of joy.

It was this Spirit that permeated the Community of the Christian Spirit and the other intentional Eucharistic communities that sprang up all those years ago. It was this Spirit that was almost completely quashed by the reactionary forces of John Paul II and Benedict XVI. This is the same Spirit that is on the rise again and is currently raising up new communities, rebuilding a church that listens to her people and guides them into the modern, secular, technological world that the static, institutional church regards as the enemy.

With the understanding that the Spirit moves in mysterious ways that are often beyond the narrow vision of the Catholic hierarchy, several questions might be asked. What if communities like CCS had not only been permitted to grow, but had also been used as a model for lay involvement and liturgical innovations for church communities throughout the archdiocese, indeed, throughout the nation, much like the reform espoused by Dutch Dominicans years later? What if the hierarchy had faith in the People of God and permitted them to design life-giving liturgies? What if priests lived among their flock, taking on their "smell," as Francis wrote, rather than separately, in an effort to preserve ontological sacredness? What if the church had issued a call to the People of God to evaluate their experiences of church in light of the world in which they lived? What if the focus of Catholic life moved from personal morality to include the repair of the world and the examination of unjust social structures? What if the People of God had been taught that the sacred, which is God, lived in them as well as in the church and in the lives of priests and that God gives all God's people divine grace, pressed down and overflowing into all laps? What if the church shook off the coils of the past and the now meaningless intricacies of ancient Greek philosophy? What if the church stopped reifying metaphors that constrain belief in God and threw off the trappings of a society that no longer exists anywhere else in the world?

The Community of the Christian Spirit was evolving into a model that could have been used to address these questions in a mature manner and grow the church into the twenty-first century. Because of fear of the institutional church, there is no existing officially sanctioned parish that will choose to ask or answer these questions, even as the People of God continue to ask them in unsanctioned reform movements like Call to Action, Future Church, and the Women's Ordination Conference, movements that are anathema to the bishops.

People who continue to worship in and financially support the institution carefully walk around the reality of potential hierarchical violence that lies just below the surface of every parish. To ask these questions publicly in an established parish when hierarchical power has declared them settled for all time is to risk not only censure, but also possible excommunication and institutional death. Rather than acting in a prophetic manner befitting Jesus, who gave not just his livelihood but also his life, clerical leaders expect their congregations to remain faithful even as the structures of domination continue to press upon them all, squeezing the very life out of the church.

It is dangerous to put God and God's creation into a straitjacket of very human construction. It is equally dangerous for one very small group of men with limited life experiences to teach that only they have the ability to image Jesus and preach the Word of God. The Word of God, the very essence of the Divine, also comes through those who have wiped children's noses and the bottoms of the elderly, through those who pick up the pieces after a disaster, and through the bodies of those who create and care for new life. There is no reason why these voices should not break open the Word in a worshipping community, adding to rather than subtracting from the many graces that exist in the entire Body of Christ rather than in one small fraction of it.

It is important for the new generation of church builders to understand that revelation did not end 2,000 years ago when the last apostle died. It did not end when the New Testament was canonized in the fourth century, and it did not end with the Council of Trent. God did not wrap divine revelation up in a package and send it to the bishop of Rome for disbursement as the ages unfolded. It does not trickle down to the People of God from the hierarchy. Revelation is humanity in all of its many and varied attributes. Revelation is, in fact, Jesus, God with us as one of us in whatever age we live.

Thus, God did not establish an unchanging, unassailable church and then throw away the plans so no one else but his trusted advisors could alter the specifications. Instead, God always makes all things new, even the Roman Catholic Church. As theologian Walter Wink wrote in his book *Engaging the Powers*, all institutions, including the Roman Catholic Church are simultaneously good, fallen, and capable of redemption and transformation.[5] All Catholics are, therefore, agents of the Roman Catholic Church's redemption and transformation into a new and more responsive entity that must walk away from its grand palaces and authoritarian mindset and, like Jesus, pitch its tent among the People of God, taking on their smell.

The plans for taking back your parish have been laid out for you. The very church that threatens to destroy your parish community empowered you at your baptism and confirmation to be an agent of change, the force of good in a troubled world. The Holy Spirit of God literally runs through your veins, and God loves you as much as God loves your bishop or your parish priest. As this book indicates, the members of the hierarchy have proven by their actions that they do not understand the holy power that is seated in the People of God and exercised in a neighborhood parish. You are the

People of God. Take matters into your own hands. The bishops will eventually follow your lead.

Epilogue

Resurrection and Ascension

"This is not a death, but the birth of a new
church and a new way of thinking."

—*Jon Rogers, co-founder of Friends*
of St. Frances X. Cabrini

In May of 2016, parishioners of St. Frances X. Cabrini in Scituate, Massachusetts, learned that the U. S. Supreme Court had
refused to hear their case. After occupying their church around the
clock for twelve years in order to save it from destruction by the
Archdiocese of Boston, they were finally forced to vacate the prem-
ises. Cardinal Sean O'Malley had previously described these faithful, loving, dedicated people as "trespassers." In reality, the people
of St. Frances X. Cabrini are prophets pointing the way to a new
model of being church.

While the Archdiocese of Boston has not publicized what it is
going to do with the property that sits upon thirty prime ocean-
front acres worth $4.2 million, the people—that is, the heart and
soul—of St. Frances X. Cabrini have moved into a Unitarian church

where they now worship, pray, and celebrate community together each Sunday without the involvement or endorsement of the Archdiocese of Boston. They continue to regard themselves as Roman Catholics.

Like Spiritus Christi, the Community of St. Peter, St. Stanislaus, St. Stephen, and any number of independent intentional Eucharistic communities, St. Frances provides Sunday Mass, the sacraments, faith formation, and spiritual guidance to its members. Like all of these communities, St. Frances is safe and welcoming to everyone.

Although the protesters were welcomed by the Archdiocese of Boston to attend other parishes—as if parishes were all the same—the Friends of St. Frances stood firm and refused to capitulate. Their hard work paid off. The Friends of St. Frances X. Cabrini parish is alive and well in its resurrected form.

Jon Rogers, co-founder of Friends of St. Frances X. Cabrini, recognized the example he and his fellow occupiers have provided to other church communities. He said, "We… are confident that other parishes in similar closure situations will build on our shoulders to carry these matters forward."[1]

And so, those who face the closing of their beloved parish should walk in faith as did their sisters and brothers at St. Frances. Fear not as the Spirit guides you into new and unfamiliar territory. The future is in your hands. Your God will be with you all the way.

This is what the Church of Jesus can look like. From the website of the Friends of St. Frances X. Cabrini:

Staying Catholic - Together!

We welcome all to worship, pray and rejoice in a Catholic community every Sunday at 10:00AM. We minister to those who have no church home, have been injured in some previous church relationship, or just want to experience Catholi-

cism. By joining us you are still a valid practicing Catholic.
The word Catholic includes more than just Roman Catholic.

Our Church Community

The Friends of St. Frances X. Cabrini strives to preach
and live the Gospel of Jesus Christ going back to the times
of Jesus. We are a church that embraces our Catholic faith.
We are the One, Holy, Catholic and Apostolic Church, which
makes us Catholic. As a community we maintain the cher-
ished traditions of the universal Catholic Church. We are a
Catholic Church community that offers the Celebration of
Mass, traditional Catholic sacraments and the Creed. Our
priests are available for Sacramental ministry including
Baptism, First Communion, Confirmation, Marriage, the
Sacrament of the Sick and Reconciliation. According to canon law, Sacraments received in our church can be registered
with your local Roman Catholic Church. We believe in faith
in action, outreach and strive to evangelize all who are seek-
ing to deepen their spiritual life. As a Catholic community
we offer an alternative for those seeking a more welcoming
Catholic experience. By joining us you are still a practicing
Catholic, but would not be supporting the Roman Catholic
Church or Archdiocese of Boston.

What We Offer

* A caring, safe and transparent Catholic Church environment * Weekly Celebration of Mass and/or Communion
Prayer Service * The Sacraments * Faith Formation - Religious Education * Youth ministry * Prayer and Spiritual
Discussion Groups *

What We Do

Practice faith in action by living as committed Catholics
Evangelize *Outreach Ministries and Programs* *

Mission Statement

The mission of The Friends of St. Frances X. Cabrini is to be a vital, loving and effective Catholic faith community, inspired by the Holy Spirit and committed to the spiritual enrichment of its parishioners through the teachings of our Lord and Savior, Jesus Christ.

The members of St. Frances believe that we have been unjustly shuttered via the flawed process of reconfiguration introduced by the Archdiocese of Boston and that this misguided decision was based solely on the value of our parish property - 30.3 acres of prime coastal real estate. We are unwavering in our commitment to reach a fair and equitable solution for the parish of St. Frances and the Archdiocese of Boston. The Friends of St. Frances are even open to discuss the option of purchasing St. Frances church, in essence purchasing our church twice.

We are resolved as disciples of Jesus Christ and as a faith community; to participate fully in the celebration of the Liturgy, to address the spiritual needs of our congregants and those in most need. Consistent with the mission of Mother Cabrini, we are committed to reaching out and offering support to all through various ministries and social programs.

The St. Frances faith family is a caring and vibrant Catholic community that welcomes all.

And this is the hope of intentional Eucharistic communities! Amen and Alleluia!

APPENDIX
PARTIAL LIST OF INTENTIONAL
EUCHARISTIC COMMUNITIES

Community of the Christian Spirit meets every Sunday at 10 a.m. for mass at the Elkins Park Shopping Center in Elkins Park, Pennsylvania. The community also meets at 5 p.m. on the third Sunday of each month (http://tuckerstales.dot5hosting.com/CCS/ccsindex. htm).

The Community of St. Mary Magdalene was founded in 2007. The community meets every Sunday at Drexel Hill United Methodist Church in Drexel Hill, Pennsylvania, and at Epworth United Methodist Church in Palmyra, NJ (www.smmagdalene.org).

Resurrection Community in Cincinnati, Ohio, was formed to support Sister Louise Akers after she was bullied by her local bishop for supporting women's ordination. The community began meeting in an Episcopal church but had to move after they were disinvited by the Episcopal bishop due to his connections with the Catholic bishop. They now meet at the United Church of Christ on the second Wednesday of each month, averaging about sixty participants.

Holy Wisdom Catholic Community began in 2012 and meets monthly at St. Luke Episcopal Church in Long Branch, California.

They gather not only for liturgy, but also to support justice and organize the community around social issues.

Compassion of Christ Community was founded in 2010. The community currently meets on the first, third, and fifth Sundays of the month at 5:00 p.m. at Prospect Park United Methodist Church, Minneapolis, Minnesota. The group shares their resources with Dignity Twin Cities, which meets on the second and fourth Sundays. Compassion of Christ belongs to an ecumenical group of local churches which sponsor Taize services, Thanksgiving services, and other prayer opportunities.

Heart of God Inclusive Catholic Community meets once a month in a house church for liturgy and hospitality in Palm Coast, Florida.

Mary Magdalene First Apostle Church meets for liturgy on the second Sunday of each month at St. John Episcopal Church in St. Cloud, Minnesota. On the fourth Sunday of the month, the community meets for meditation and discussion on specific topics.

The Community of St. Bridget, an inclusive Catholic community, meets every Saturday at 5 p.m. for liturgy at Brecksville United Church of Christ, 23 Public Square, Brecksville, OH 44141 (http://www.communityofstbridget.org/).

Mary, Mother of Jesus Inclusive Catholic Community meets every Saturday at 4:00 p.m. at St. Andrew UCC Church in Sarasota, Florida.

Living Beatitudes was started by Dignity Dayton forty years ago. They meet in an Episcopal church in downtown Dayton, Ohio.

All Are One Roman Catholic Community meets in Winona, Minnesota, at the Lutheran Campus Center on the campus of the Winona State University every Sunday at 10:00 a.m. They also have a monthly Saturday evening Mass. The community engages in various social justice ministries.

Living Water Inclusive Catholic Community meets weekly in Baltimore, Annapolis, and in the central counties of Maryland in several rented churches. They are engaged in various peace and justice activities and engage in charitable giving to social welfare agencies (livingwatercommunity@comcast.net).

New Jerusalem Community has been meeting monthly since 2012 in Wilmington, Delaware.

St. Anthony's Intentional Community meets each Sunday morning at 9:30 a.m. and on Wednesdays at 1 p.m. The community serves Santa Barbara, Ventura, Oxnard, and Ojai in California. St. Anthony is located at St. Anthony's Chapel (behind the Santa Barbara mission) 2300 Garden St., Santa Barbara, CA 93105 (http://stanthony-community.org). The community is over forty years old.

Holy Wisdom Inclusive Catholic Community meets for Mass at 5:00 p.m. on the second and fourth Saturdays of the month at Saint Benedict's Episcopal Church in Lacey, Washington. We continue each Eucharist with a potluck. To learn more, please see our website: www.holywisdomicc.org.

St Praxedis Catholic Community in New York City meets for mass on the second Saturday of the month at the Assembly Hall of the Judson Memorial Church in the West Village of Manhattan. They also meet on the third Sunday of the month at The Commons on Atlantic Avenue in downtown Brooklyn (StpraxedisCatholicCommunity. org).

Sophia Christi Catholic Community in Portland, Oregon, meets the second Saturday of the month for Mass at 5:00 p.m., followed by potluck community dinner. They meet at Northminster Presbyterian Church, 2823 N. Rosa Parks Way, Portland, OR 97217.

Catholic Church of the Beatitudes in Santa Barbara, California, meets every Saturday at 4:30 p.m. at the First Congregational Church at 2101 State St. (corner of Padre and State). The community is new way of being Roman Catholic through Worship and Service in our local community. For information and/or contacting Pastoral Team please visit our website at: www.beatitudes-sb.org.

Upper Room Inclusive Catholic Community meets weekly at 10:00 a.m. at the New Covenant Presbyterian Church, 916 Western Avenue, Albany, New York. For more information, please visit our website at: http://www.inclusivecatholiccommunity-nycr.org/ or send an email to: upperroomicc@gf1mail.com.

Wood River Inclusive Catholic Community meets for Mass and the celebration of Sacraments on Sunday evenings 7:00 p.m. at Light on the Mountains Spiritual Center, 12446 State Highway 75, Ketchum, ID 83340.

Mary of Magdala, Apostle to the Apostle meets in Wauwatosa, Wisconsin.

Mary Magdalene Apostle Catholic Community meets for weekly liturgies at 2696 Melbourne Drive, San Diego, CA 92123.

Holy Spirit Catholic Community, an inclusive Vatican II Roman Catholic Church where are welcome at the table meets for Mass on Saturdays at 4:30 p.m. and Sundays at 5:30 p.m. at 3925 West Central Avenue (Washington Church Chapel), Toledo, OH 43606 (www.holyspirittoledo.org).

Sophia Inclusive Catholic Community was founded in September 2008. The community gathers for Eucharistic celebration every Sunday at 10:00 a.m., at The Center, 65 Newton Sparta Road, Newton, NJ 07860. In the tradition of early church communities, all are welcome at the table in this discipleship of equals (http://sophiainclusivecatholiccommunity.org).

St. Mary of Magdala Church in Harwich Port (Cape Cod), Massachusetts, is an Ecumenical Catholic Community that gathers for worship each Sunday at 10:00 a.m. in St. Mary of Magdala Chapel at Evensong Retreat Center in Harwich Port, Massachusetts. The community is Catholic in their heritage and worship, moving forward with the teachings of the Second Vatican Council. They are ecumenical in their makeup and outreach (revmariedavid@gmail.com).

Oscar Romero Church is an inclusive church in the Catholic tradition that meets in the dining room of the Rochester Catholic Worker house, St. Joseph's House of Hospitality. They celebrate a Spanish-language Mass in migrant camps outside of Rochester (www.saintjoeshouse.org).

The Spirit of Life Community meets every Sunday in the Congregational Church of Weston, Massachusetts. Mass begins at 4:00 p.m. (fall and winter) and 5:00 p.m. (spring and summer) (www.SpiritofLifeCommunity.org).

The Good Shepherd Inclusive Catholic Community of Fort Myers, Florida, is a rainbow community of people of all races, ages, sexual orientations, and socioeconomic status serving the community and worshiping God together. They also offer a Hospitality House as a temporary respite for members in danger of homelessness. Good Shepherd Community is presently. Call (239) 565-6173 for further details and Mass times.

Inclusive Catholic Community is a small house church that celebrates a Eucharistic liturgy every Sunday in the home of the presiding pastor. We celebrate the sacraments, including weddings and baptisms. (631) 725-8093.

Sophia Christi Catholic Community in Eugene, Oregon, meets the 2nd Sunday of the month for Mass at 4:00pm followed by potluck community dinner at First Congregational Church, 1050 E. 23rd Ave., Eugene, OR 97405.

An **ecumenical group** meets on the 2nd and 4th Sundays of the month at 10 a.m. at Park Health and Rehab Center, a nursing home in St. Louis Park, 4415 - 36 1/2 Street. St Louis Park is a suburb of Minneapolis.

CANADIAN COMMUNITIES

Mary of Magdala Inclusive Catholic Community in Regina, Saskatchewan, Canada, meet as a house church the 2nd weekend of the month and for special occasions such as Christmas and the Easter Triduum. Contact Jane Kryzanowski, RCWP at photina61@gmail.com for further details.

Our Lady of Guadalupe Tonantzin Community holds liturgies at 3:00 p.m. on the first and third Sundays of the month at The Listening Post, 382 Main Street, Vancouver, British Columbia, Canada. We are committed to ministries of environmental justice and reconciliation between Aboriginals and non-aboriginals at the local level.

Sourdough house church in Sudbury, Ontario, meets for Eucharist on the third Sunday of the month at 10 a.m. in my home, 568 Grandview Blvd. The French-speaking community meets for Eucharist on the third Thursday of the month at 10 a.m., a "movable feast." We meet in one another's homes.

St. Brigid of Kildare Catholic Faith Community meets in Calgary, Alberta, on the second Sunday of each month, at 10 a.m., at Kingsland Community Centre (505 78th Ave. S.W., Calgary) and on the third Wednesday evening of each month at 7 p.m. (except December, July, and August) for an education/discussion evening (www.saintbrigids.org; Contact: hearthkeepers@saintbrigids.org).

NOTES

PROLOGUE: SINGING A NEW SONG

1. Roberta Brunner, *"A History of the Community of the Christian Spirit,"* unpublished manuscript.

INTRODUCTION: DYSTOPIAN MYOPIA

1. John W. O'Malley, *What Happened at Vatican II* (Boston: Harvard University Press, 2010).

2. Maike Hickson, "Pope Emeritus Benedict breaks silence: speaks of deep crisis facing Church post-Vatican II," *Life Site*, March 16, 2016, https://www.lifesitenews.com/news/pope-emeritus-benedict-says-church-is-now-facing-a-two-sided-deep-crisis.

3. Michael O' Loughlin, "Pew Survey: Percentage of US Catholics drops and Catholicism is losing members faster than any denomination," *Crux*, May 12, 2015, http://www.chicagomanualofstyle.org/tools_citationguide.html.

4. Jones et al., *Exodus: Why Americans Are Leaving Religion—and Why They're Unlikely to Come Back* (Washington D.C.: Public Religion Research Institute, 2016), accessed on July 17, 2017, https://www.prri.org/wp-content/uploads/2016/09/PRRI-RNS-Unaffiliated-Report.pdf.

5. Christa Pongratz-Lippitt, "Pope Francis Discusses Married Priests, Women Deacons with German newspaper," *National Catholic Reporter*, March 10, 2017, https://www.ncronline.org/news/vatican/pope-francis-discusses-married-priests-women-deacons-german-newspaper.

6. Alfred Lubrano, "Anger Over Plans To Sell Church," *Philadelphia* Inquirer. 6- 13-16, accessed on July 17, 2017, at *Black Christian News Network 1*, http://blackchristiannews.com/2016/06/battle-over-sale-of-phillys-first-black-catholic-church-intensifies/.

7. Jason Horowitz, "Steve Bannon Carries Battle to Another Influential Hub: The Vatican," *New York Times*, February 7, 2017, https://www.nytimes.com/2017/02/07/world/europe/vatican-steve-bannon-pope-francis.html.

CHAPTER ONE: OPERATION CHAOS

1. John T. McGreevy, *Parish Boundaries* (Chicago: University of Chicago Press. 1996), p. 5.

2. McGreevey, *Parish Boundaries*, p. 83.

3. Gordon Whitman and Anne B. Shlay, *Uneven Development* (Philadelphia: Research for Democracy. September, 2004), p. v–11.

4. Patrick Hildebrandt, "New AD Directive is a Call to Arms," *Philadelphia Church Project*, January 11, 2016, http://www.phillychurchproject.com/project-blog/2016/1/10/new-ad-announcement-is-a-call-to-arms.

5. Anthony Cardinal Bevilacqua, "Healing Racism through Faith and Truth," *National Catholic Register*, June 21, 1998, http://www.ncregister.com/site/article/healing_racism_through_faith_and_truth.

6. Richard K. Taylor, "Synod Topical Commission on Moral and Social Issues: Document Comparison of Racism Section" (unpublished work, 2002).

7. Brigid Sweeney, "A Catholic Reformation," *Crain's Chicago Business*, July 25, 2016, http://www.chicagobusiness.com/section/catholic.

8. Mark M. Gray, "Checkup Time," *1964*, accessed June 8, 2014, http://nineteensixty-four.blogspot.com/2014/07/checkup-time.html.

9. Kenneth Gavin, "Archdiocese Announces Parish Mergers in Philadelphia as well as Delaware, Montgomery and Bucks Counties Resulting from Pastoral Planning Initiative," *Archdiocese of Philadelphia*, June 1, 2014, http://archphila.org/press%20releases/pr002376.php.

10. Joel Landau et al., "Catholic Archdiocese of New York to merge 112 parishes into 55 new congregations," *Daily News*, November 3, 2014, http://www.nydailynews.com/new-york/archdiocese-new-york-merge-55-parishes-report-article-1.1996146.

11. Sharon Otterman, "Heartache for New York's Catholics as Church Closings Are Announced," *New York Times*, November 2, 2014, https://www.nytimes.com/2014/11/03/nyregion/new-york-catholics-are-set-to-learn-fate-of-their-parishes.html.

12. Manya Brachear Pashman, "Massive overhaul slated for Chicago Archdiocese," *Chicago Tribune*, February 7, 2016, http://www.chicagotribune.com/news/ct-archdiocese-parish-reorganization-met-20160205-story.html.

13. Pam Belluck, "Archdiocese in Boston Plans to Close 65 Catholic Parishes by the End of the Year," *New York Times,* May 26, 2004, http://www.nytimes.com/2004/05/26/us/archdiocese-in-boston-plans-to-close-65-catholic-parishes-by-the-end-of-the-year.html?_r=0.

14. Jonathan Finer, "The Faithful Stand Guard Over Church Near Boston," *The Washington Post,* September 10, 2004, http://www.washingtonpost.com/wp-dyn/articles/A9810-2004Sep9.html.

15. Justin Engel, "Diocese of Saginaw to reduce services at 53 of 109 churches across mid-Michigan," *Mlive,* January 20, 2013, http://www.mlive.com/news/bay-city/index.ssf/2013/01/diocese_of_saginaw_to_reduce_s.html.

16. "Camden Bishop Reduces Church Consolidation," *ABC Action News,* August 27, 2008, http://6abc.com/archive/6353796/.

17. Maryann Gogniat Eidemiller, "Closed parishes' sacred goods put to use at other churches," *OSV Newsweekly,* accessed on July 18, 2012, https://www.osv.com/OSVNewsweekly/Story/TabId/2672/ArtMID/13567/ArticleID/2095/Closed-parishes-sacred-goods-put-to-use-at-other-churches.aspx.

18. Michael deCourcy Hinds, "Schools and Churches Close, Angering Catholics," *New York Times,* accessed on July 5, 1993, http://www.nytimes.com/1993/07/05/us/schools-and-churches-close-angering-catholics.html.

19. Mike Bell, "Sioux City Diocese unveils plan to reduce parishes from 108 to 67," *Sioux City Journal,* February 26, 2016, http://siouxcityjournal.com/news/local/sioux-city-diocese-unveils-plan-to-reduce-parishes-from-to/article_888aa8d5-fab6-5e70-9eda-132621a4b759.html.

20. Deacon Keith Fournier, "52 Parishes to Close in the Diocese of Cleveland; Major Restructuring Underway," *Catholic Online,* March 15, 2009, http://www.catholic.org/news/national/story.php?id=32595.

21. Christa Pongratz-Lippitt, "German Priests: Open the Priesthood to Women, Make Priestly Celibacy Optional," *National Catholic Reporter,* January 13, 2017, https://www.ncronline.org/blogs/german-priests-open-priesthood-women-make-priestly-celibacy-voluntary.

22. Thomas Tobin, "Let's be honest: It's a lack of faith," *National Catholic Reporter,* March 20, 2017, https://www.ncronline.org/blogs/ncr-today/lets-be-honest-its-lack-faith.

23. Donna C. Day, "Church-based Community Organizing: Philadelphia Perspectives," *COMM-ORG,* accessed on July 18, 2017, https://comm-org.wisc.edu/papers98/warren/faith/day.html.

24. Interview with former pastor Herbert Brevard in 2002.

25. Peter Feuerherd, "Opponents challenge parish closings, mergers, in NY archdiocese," *National Catholic Reporter*, September 23, 2015, https://www.ncronline.org/news/faith-parish/opponents-challenge-parish-closings-mergers-ny-archdiocese.

26. Debora Fougere, "Anger grows at NY archdiocese for closing dozens of churches," *Al Jazeera*, July 29, 2015, http://america.aljazeera.com/articles/2015/7/29/anger-grows-ny-archdiocese-closing-churches.html.

27. Joshua McElwee, "Cardinal Dolan contemplates selling NY chancery in biting letter to priests," *National Catholic Reporter*, January 11, 2017, https://www.ncronline.org/news/vatican/cardinal-dolan-contemplates-selling-ny-chancery-biting-letter-priests.

28. Susan Coleman, "Letters," *National Catholic Reporter*, February 10, 2017.

29. Laura Sanicola and Corky Siemaszko, "Locksmiths descend on Our Lady of Peace during its last Mass before the beloved East Side church shutters," *New York Daily News*, August 1, 2015, http://www.nydailynews.com/new-york/locksmiths-descend-lady-peace-mass-article-1.2311109.

30. *Catechism of the Catholic Church* (New York: Doubleday), n. 2426.

31. Matt. 6:24 (New International Version).

32. Kristin E. Holmes, "Mergers rip through Conshohocken parishes," *The Inquirer*, February 15, 2015, http://www.philly.com/philly/news/pennsylvania/montgomery/20150215_Mergers_rip_through_Conshohocken_parishes.html.

33. Manya Brashear Pashman, "Massive overhaul slated for Chicago Archdiocese," *Chicago Tribune*, February 7, 2016, http://www.chicagotribune.com/news/ct-archdiocese-parish-reorganization-met-20160205-story.html.

34. Brigid Sweeney, "A Catholic Reformation," *Crain's Chicago Business*, July 25, 2016, http://www.chicagobusiness.com/section/catholic.

35. Natasha Lindstrom, "Reviews imminent for struggling Roman Catholic parishes in Pittsburgh diocese," *The Tribune-Review*, April 26, 2016, http://triblive.com/news/allegheny/10371846-74/parishes-diocese-pittsburgh.

CHAPTER TWO: THE MAGIC CHRISTIANS

1. Betty Clermont, "Vatican Corruption, Media Dysfunction, Pope Still the 4th Most Powerful Person in the World," *Daily Kos*, November 22, 2015, https://www.dailykos.com/story/2015/11/22/1452850/-Vatican-Corruption-Media-Dysfunction-Pope-Still-the-4th-Most-Powerful-Person-in-the-World.

2. Gianluigi Nuzzi, *Merchants in the Temple* (New York: Henry Holt and Co., 2015), p. 4.

3. Nuzzi, *Merchants in the Temple*, p. 9–12.

4. Gaia Pianigiani, "Vatican Finds Stash of Money Tucked Away," *New York Times*, December 4, 2014, https://www.nytimes.com/2014/12/05/world/europe/vatican-finds-hundreds-of-millions-of-euros-tucked-away.html.

5. "German archdiocese of Cologne reveals 3.8 billion dollar fortune," *DailyMail.com.*, February 18, 2015, http://www.dailymail.co.uk/wires/ap/article-2958552/German-archdiocese-Cologne-reveals-3-8-billion-fortune.html.

6. Carol Glatz, "Archbishop says Vatican officials are 'ashamed to tell people' where they work," *The Catholic Herald*, January 15, 2016, http://www.catholicherald.co.uk/news/2016/01/15/archbishop-says-vatican-officials-are-ashamed-to-tell-people-where-they-work/.

7. Philip Willan, "How the Vatican sold its soul," *The Guardian*, June 3, 2009, https://www.theguardian.com/commentisfree/belief/2009/jun/03/vatican-central-bank.

8. Davide Casati, "Of Virtue, Vice, and a Vatican Priest," *New York Times*, October 18,2014, https://www.nytimes.com/2014/10/19/business/of-virtue-and-vice-and-a-vatican-priest.html.

9. Barbie Latza Nadeau, "Hospital Funds Diverted to Cardinal's Villa," *Daily Beast*, April 3, 2016, http://www.thedailybeast.com/hospital-funds-diverted-to-cardinals-villa.

10. Glatz, "Archbishop says Vatican officials are 'ashamed to tell people' where they work."

11. "The Catholic Church in America: Earthly concerns," *The Economist*, April 18, 2012, http://www.economist.com/node/21560536.

12. Ralph Cipriano, "Lavish spending in Archdiocese skips inner city," *National Catholic Reporter*, June 19, 1998, http://natcath.org/NCR_Online/archives2/1998b/061998/061998a.htm.

13. Jason Berry, *Render Unto Rome: The Secret Life of Money in the Catholic Church* (New York: Crown Publishers, 2011), p. 252.

14. Daniel Burke, "The lavish homes of American archbishops," *CNN*, August 3, 2014, http://religion.blogs.cnn.com/2014/08/03/the-lavish-homes-of-american-archbishops/.

15. Mauro Bazzucchi, "While Pope Francis Lives in a Dorm, U. S. Bishops Enjoy Italian Luxury," *HuffPost*, March 5, 2016, http://www.huffingtonpost.com/entry/us-bishops-italy-residence-luxuryf_us_56cf696de4b0bf0dab315eba.

16. https://www.usnews.com/news/world/articles/2017-02-18/
    Vatican-froze-two-million-euros-in-suspect-funds-in-2016.

17. Michael W. Ryan, "The Second Greatest Scandal in the Church: Priests
    & Lay Leaders Stealing from the Sunday Collection," *New Oxford Review*,
    September 2003, accessed on July 9, 2017, at ChurchSecurity.info, http://
    www.churchsecurity.info/Scandal2.pdf.

18. Rod Dreher."Weakland's Exit: A liberal bishop and his downfall," *National Review*, May 24, 2002, accessed on July 9, 2017, at Free Republic,
    http://www.freerepublic.com/focus/news/689151/posts?page=8.

19. Michael Powell, "At 75, a Battle-Tested but Unwavering Cardinal,"
    New York Times, April 23, 2007, http://www.nytimes.com/2007/04/23/
    nyregion/23egan.html.

20. Jack Ruhl and Diane Ruhl, "NCR research: Costs of sex
    abuse crisis to US church underestimated," November 2,
    2015, https://www.ncronline.org/news/accountability/
    ncr-research-costs-sex-abuse-crisis-us-church-underestimated.

21. "The Catholic Church in America: Earthly Concerns," *The Economist*,
    August 18, 2012.

22. Sharon Otterman, "Archdiocese of New York Seeks $100 Million
    Mortgage for Sexual Abuse Fund," *The New York Times*, February 28,
    2017, https://www.nytimes.com/2017/02/28/nyregion/archdiocese-
    sexual-abuse-fund-mortgage.html.

23. "Frequently Requested Church Statistics," *Center for Applied Research in the Apostolate*, http://cara.georgetown.edu/
    frequently-requested-church-statistics/.

24. Patsy McGarry, "Papal nuncio warns Catholics against becom-
    ing 'caricatures,'" *The Irish Times*, August, 22, 2015, https://
    www.irishtimes.com/news/social-affairs/religion-and-beliefs/
    papal-nuncio-warns-catholics-against-becoming-caricatures-1.2324952.

25. "Frequently Requested Church Statistics," *Center for Applied Research in the Apostolate*, http://cara.georgetown.edu/
    frequently-requested-church-statistics/.

26. "Facts about the Priest Shortage, Optional Celibacy, and Women's
    Roles in the Church," *Future Church*, accessed on July 9, 2017, https://
    www.futurechurch.org/future-of-priestly-ministry/optional-celibacy/
    facts-about-priest-shortage-optional-celibacy-and.

27. "A Report of the Thirty-Seventh Statewide Investigating Grand
    Jury," *Commonwealth of Pennsylvania, Office of Attorney General*,
    accessed on July 19, 2017, http://www.bishop-accountability.org/
    reports/2016_03_01_Pennsylvania_Grand_Jury_Report_on_Diocese_
    of_Altoona_Johnstown.pdf.

28. Joshua McElwee, "Cardinal Cupich shoulders Chicago's Catholic future," *The National Catholic Reporter*, December 5, 2016, https://www.ncronline.org/news/people/cardinal-cupich-shoulders-chicagos-catholic-future.

29. *A New Vision, 2016*, (Philadelphia: Catholic Charities Appeal, 2016), https://www.catholiccharitiesappeal.org/files/5214/5401/8577/CCA_16LeadBrochure.final.pdf.

30. Christa Pongratz-Lippitt, "Brazil may soon have married priests, says Leonardo Boff," *National Catholic Reporter*, December 30, 2016, https://www.ncronline.org/news/vatican/brazil-may-soon-have-married-priests-says-leonardo-boff.

31. Tom Roberts, "Australian priests offer support for deposed bishop," *National Catholic Reporter*, May 3, 2011, https://www.ncronline.org/news/vatican/australian-priests-offer-support-deposed-bishop.

32. Christa Pongratz-Lippitt, "German priests: open the priesthood to women, make priestly celibacy optional," *National Catholic Reporter*, January 13, 2017, https://www.ncronline.org/blogs/german-priests-open-priesthood-women-make-priestly-celibacy-voluntary.

33. Tré Goins-Phillips, "New study reveals what most Americans believe about female pastors, priests," *The Blaze*, March 15, 2017, http://www.theblaze.com/news/2017/03/15/new-study-reveals-what-most-americans-believe-about-female-pastors-priests/.

34. Michael Lipka, "U.S. Catholics more hopeful than expectant of changes to Church teachings," *Pew Research Center*, March 12, 2014, http://www.pewresearch.org/fact-tank/2014/03/12/u-s-catholics-more-hopeful-than-expectant-of-changes-to-church-teachings/.

Chapter Three: Control

1. "Q & A with Sister Kate Kuenstler," *Global Sisters Report*, November 15, 2016, https://globalsistersreport.org/plus1/vote/node/43331/plus1_node_vote?token=n9AJlcV7chW06d1QOn877Gn7-_MjmX0ppZh_GYVtAsQ&destination=node/43331.

2. Berry, *Render Unto Rome*, p. 94.

3. Berry, *Render Unto Rome*, p. 114.

4. Kristin Holmes, "Mergers rip through Conshohocken parishes," *Phily.com*, February 15, 2015, http://www.philly.com/philly/news/pennsylvania/montgomery/20150215_Mergers_rip_through_Conshohocken_parishes.html.

5. Sharon Otterman, "Feelings of Betrayal after Catholic Church is Leased to Coptic Parish," *The New York Times*, March 5, 2017, https://www.nytimes.com/2017/03/05/nyregion/feelings-of-betrayal-after-catholic-church-is-leased-to-coptic-parish.html.

6. Berry, *Render Unto Rome*. p. 34.

7. Phillip Marcello, "Parishioners Fight AD of Boston for Control of Closed Churches." *Portland Press Herald*, June 10, 2015.

8. Margaret Bernstein, "Some Catholic Church Appeals To Keep Parishes Open Denied," *Plain Dealer*, April 22, 209.

9. Patrick Hildebrandt, "New AD Directive is a Call to Arms," *Philadelphia Church Project*, January 11, 2016, ttp://www.phillychurchproject.com/project-blog/2016/1/10/new-ad-announcement-is-a-call-to-arms.

10. https://www.futurechurch.org/sites/default/files/2003-natl-study-parish-reorg.pdf. p.22

11. Peter Borre, https://peterborre.com/.

12. Lubrano, "Anger Over Plans To Sell Church."

13. "Crisis Kit," *Future Church*, accessed on Jul 11, 2017, https://www.futurechurch.org/save-our-parish-community/save-our-parish-community/resource/crisis-kit.

14. *Code of Canon Law*, 1752, accessed on July 11, 2017, http://www.vatican.va/archive/ENG1104/_P70.HTM.

15. "Crisis Kit," *Future Church*.

16. Maura Grunlund, "Vatican Appeals could keep Staten Island Roman Catholic churches open," *silive.com*, January 20, 2014, http://www.silive.com/news/2014/01/hold_for_monday_making_all_thi.html.

17. Kate Kuenstler, "Commentary on Decrees from the Congregation for Clergy Upholding Petition for Recourse Made by Thirteen Parishes of the Cleveland Diocese," *St. Casimir Parish*, accessed on July 12, 2017, http://www.stcasimir.com/Commentary%20on%20Cleveland%20Decrees%203-29-12.pdf.

18. James A. Coriden, "A Challenge: Making the Rights Real, " *Association for the Rights of Catholics in the Church*, accessed July 19, 2017, http://www.arcc-catholic-rights.net/making_rights_real.htm.

19. *Code of Canon Law*, 208–221.

20. Tony Flannery, "I Am Celebrating a Public Mass on January 22nd: You Are Welcome to Come if You Wish," accessed on July 12, 2017, http://www.tonyflannery.com/i-am-celebrating-a-public-mass-on-january-22nd-you-are-welcome-to-come-if-you-wish/.

Chapter Four: The Dragon's Game

1. Theodor Klauser, *A Short History of the Western Liturgy* (London: Oxford University Press, 1965) p. 34.

2. Ignatius of Antioch, "Epistle of Ignatius to the Smyrnaeans," *New Advent*, accessed on July 13, 2017, http://www.newadvent.org/fathers/0109.htm.

3. Trip Gabriel, "Pennsylvania Priest Accused of Abuse Was Reported 5 Years Ago, Records Show," *New York Times*, September 26, 2014, https://www.nytimes.com/2014/09/27/us/priest-in-sexual-abuse-case-was-reported-to-diocese-5-years-ago-records-show.html.

4. Abby Ohlheiser, "A Catholic Archbishop Claims He Wasn't Sure Whether Sexual Abuse of Kids Was a Crime," *The Atlantic*, June 10, 2014, https://www.theatlantic.com/national/archive/2014/06/a-catholic-archbishop-claims-he-wasnt-sure-whether-sexual-abuse-of-kids-was-a-crime/372490/.

5. Jane Musgrave, "Priest sues diocese, claims it punished him for reporting sex abuse." *Palm Beach Post*, January 11, 2017, http://www.mypalmbeachpost.com/news/crime--law/priest-sues-diocese-claiming-punished-him-for-reporting-sex-abuse/eB6segzLBqLrAwrdpgOxTN/.

6. Stephanie Kirchgaessner and Amanda Holpuch, "How cardinal disgraced in Boston child abuse scandal found a Vatican haven," *The Guardian*, November 6, 2015, https://www.theguardian.com/world/2015/nov/06/cardinal-bernard-law-disgraced-boston-child-abuse-scandal-vatican-haven-spotlight.

7. "Legionaries of Christ Denounce Founder, Marcial Maciel Degollado," *New York Times*, February 6, 2014, https://www.nytimes.com/2014/02/07/world/legionaries-of-christ-denounce-founder-marcial-maciel-degollado.html.

8. Cedar Attanasio, "Child Abuse In Church: How Pedophile Jozef Wesolowski Could Live Like The Pope After Dominican Scandal," *Latin Times*, June 16, 2015, http://www.latintimes.com/child-abuse-church-how-pedophile-jozef-wesolowski-could-live-pope-after-dominican-322903.

9. "Chile: Catholics Demand Pope Fire Bishop Complicit in Sex Abuse," *Telesur*, February 7, 2016, http://www.telesurtv.net/english/news/Chile-Catholics-Demand-Pope-Fire-Bishop-Complicit-in-Sex-Abuse-20160207-0036.html.

10. Marie Collins, "Exclusive: Survivor explains decision to leave Vatican abuse commission," *National Catholic Reporter*, March 1, 2017, https://www.ncronline.org/news/people/exclusive-survivor-explains-decision-leave-vaticans-abuse-commission.

11. Luke 4:18–19.

Chapter Five: The Crack

1. "Welcome: About Spiritus," *Spiritus Christi*, accessed on July 15, 2017, http://www.spirituschristi.org/welcome/about-spiritus/?view=mobile.

2. "About Us: 2008-02-24 Statement of the Community of St. Stephen's," *Spirit of St. Stephen's Catholic Community*, accessed on July 15, 2017, http://www.spiritofststephens.org/aboutus/91-formation-from-st-stephens-parish/635-2008-2-24-statement-of-the-community-of-st-stephens.

3. Jon Tevlin, "'We're Taking On Water,' and New Priest Knows He Can't Walk on It," *Star Tribune*, February 15, 2009, accessed at The Wild Reed on July 15, 2017, http://thewildreed.blogspot.com/2009/02/catholic-crisis-and-opportunity-in.html.

4. Regina Brett, "St. Peter split from diocese symbolizes defining moment for all Catholics," *Cleveland Plain Dealer*, August 22, 2010, http://www.cleveland.com/brett/blog/index.ssf/2010/08/a_defining_moment_for_catholic.html .

5. Michael O'Malley, "Parishioners, priest from closed St. Peter Catholic Church defy bishop, celebrate Mass in new home," *The Plain Dealer*, August, 16, 2010, http://blog.cleveland.com/metro/2010/08/parishioners_from_closed_catho.html.

6. Tim Townsend, "Ab Wants St. Stan Priest Defrocked," *St. Louis Post-Dispatch*, January 15, 208.

7. Malcom Gay, "Defiant St. Louis Church Wins Archdiocese Suit," *New York Times*, March 17, 2012. http://www.nytimes.com/2012/03/18/us/defiant-st-louis-church-wins-archdiocese-suit.html.

8. "The Church and the Ministry," p. 5.

9. Robert McClory. "The Dutch Plan: Will Innovation Save This Church?" *National Catholic Reporter*, December 14, 2007, http://natcath.org/NCR_Online/archives2/2007d/121407/121407a.htm.

10. Michael O'Malley, "Excommunicated Church Thrives Despite Censure." *Huffington Post*. April 17, 2011, http://www.huffingtonpost.com/2011/04/17/excommunicated-church-thr_n_846339.html.

Chapter Six: Dandelion Seeds

1. Matt. 7:16.

2. David Gibson, "Archbishop Chaput welcomes a 'smaller church' of holier Catholics," *National Catholic Reporter*, October 21, 2016.

CHAPTER SEVEN: TECTONICS

1. Rom. 1, 16:3–4, 10-11;

2. Rom. 16:1–16.

3. Gal. 3:28–29.

4. Josef Jungmann, *The Early Liturgy* (South Bend: University of Notre Dame Press, 1959), p. 17.

5. John Dick, "A Conversation about Church and Community," *Another Voice*, February 18, 2007, https://anothervoice-greenleaf. org/2017/02/18/a-conversation-about-church-and-community/.

6. Cox, Stephen, *American Christianity*, Austin, University of Texas Press, 2014, p. 11.

7. Joseph Martos, *Deconstructing Sacramental Theology and Reconstructing Catholic Ritual* (Eugene, Oregon: Wipf and Stock Publishers, 2015), p. 282.

8. Dan Stockman, "Former LCWR President: Communities must embrace the shift in religious life," *Global Sisters Report*, October 14, 2016, http://globalsistersreport.org/news/trends/former-lcwr-president-communities-must-embrace-shift-religious-life-42726.

9. Delores Dufner, "Sing a New Church," *OCP*, 1991, https://www.ocp.org/en-us/products/9922/sing-a-new-church.

CHAPTER EIGHT: THE ADULT DANCE

1. Michael O'Malley, "Cleveland Catholic Diocese announces church closures," *The Plain Dealer*, March 13, 2009, http://blog.cleveland.com/metro/2009/03/parishioners_in_the_cleveland.html.

2. Berry, *Render Unto Rome*, p. 199.

CHAPTER NINE: UPSIDE DOWN

1. Peter Feuerherd, "North Carolina 'Church in Exile' battles restorationists," *National Catholic Reporter*, January 26, 2017, https://www.ncronline.org/blogs/ncr-today/north-carolina-church-exile-battles-restorationists.

2. Robert McClory, "Hermeneutics as Weapon," *National Catholic Reporter*, August 26, 2011, https://www.ncronline.org/blogs/ncr-today/hermeneutics-weapon.

3. Acts 2:17–18.

4. Michael Morwood, *Tomorrow's Catholic* (Mystic: Twenty-Third Publications, 1997), p. 39.

5. Walter Wink, *Engaging the Powers: Discernment and Resistance in the World of Domination* (Minneapolis: Fortress Press, 1992), p. 199.

EPILOGUE: RESURRECTION AND ASCENSION

1. Mark Labbe, "Group says it will end vigil at closed Scituate church," *The Pilot*, May 16, 2016, http://www.thebostonpilot.com/article.asp?ID=176493#.

BIBLIOGRAPHY

"About Us: 2008-02-24 Statement of the Community of St. Stephen's." *Spirit of St. Stephen's Catholic Community.* Accessed on July 15, 2017. http://www. spiritofststephens.org/aboutus/91-formation-from-st-stephens-parish/635-2008-2-24-statement-of-the-community-of-st-stephens.

Anderson, Travis, Martin Finucane, and John R. Ellement. "Supreme Court declines to hear Scituate parishioners' case." *Boston Globe.* May 16, 2016. https://www.bostonglobe.com/metro/2016/05/16/supreme-declines-hear-case-scituate-parishioners-fighting-church-closure/zFXcSCb2afoucZ2WpwpPnK/story.html.

Attanasio, Cedar. "Child Abuse In Church: How Pedophile Jozef Wesolowski Could Live Like The Pope After Dominican Scandal." *Latin Times.* June 16, 2015. http://www.latintimes.com/child-abuse-church-how-pedophile-jozef-wesolowski-could-live-pope-after-dominican-322903.

Bazzucchi, Mauro. "While Pope Francis Lives in a Dorm, U. S. Bishops Enjoy Italian Luxury." *HuffPost.* March 4, 2016. http://www.huffingtonpost.com/entry/us-bishops-italy-residence-luxuryf_us_56cf696de4b0bf0dab315eba.

Bell, Mike. "Sioux City Diocese unveils plan to reduce parishes from 108 to 67." *Sioux City Journal.* February 26, 2016. http://siouxcityjournal.com/news/local/sioux-city-diocese-unveils-plan-to-reduce-parishes-from-to/article_888aa8d5-fab6-5e70-9eda-132621a4b759.html.

Belluck, Pam. "Archdiocese in Boston Plans to Close 65 Catholic Parishes by the End of the Year." *New York Times.* May 26, 2004. http://www.nytimes.com/2004/05/26/us/archdiocese-in-boston-plans-to-close-65-catholic-parishes-by-the-end-of-the-year.html?_r=0.

Bernstein, Margaret. "Some Catholic Church Appeals To Keep Parishes Open Denied." *Plain Dealer*. April 22, 2009. http://blog.cleveland.com/metro/2009/04/some_catholic_church_appeals_d.html.

Berry, Jason. *Render Unto Rome: The Secret Life of Money in the Catholic Church*. New York: Crown Publishers. 2011.

Bevilacqua, Anthony. "Healing Racism through Faith and Truth." *National Catholic Register*. June 21, 1998. http://www.ncregister.com/site/article/healing_racism_through_faith_and_truth.

Borre, Peter. *A topnotch WordPress.com site*. https://peterborre.com/.

Brett, Regina. "St. Peter Split From Diocese Symbolizes Defining Moment For all Catholics." *The Plain Dealer*. August 22 2010. http://www.cleveland.com/brett/blog/index.ssf/2010/08/a_defining_moment_for_catholic.html.

Brunner, Roberta. "A History of the Community of the Christian Spirit." Unpublished manuscript.

Burke, Daniel. "The Lavish Homes of American Bishops." *CNN*. Accessed on July 19, 2017. http://www.cnn.com/interactive/2014/08/us/american-archbishops-lavish-homes/index.html.

Byrne, Julie. *The Other Catholics: Remaking America's Largest Religion*. New York: Columbia University Press. 2016.

"Camden Bishop Reduces Church Consolidation." *ABC Action News*. August 27, 2008. http://6abc.com/archive/6353796/.

Casati, Davide. "Of Virtue and Vice, and a Vatican Priest." *New York Times*. October 18, 2014. https://www.nytimes.com/2014/10/19/business/of-virtue-and-vice-and-a-vatican-priest.html?login=email.

Catechism of the Catholic Church. New York: Doubleday. 1995.

"The Catholic Church in America: Earthly concerns." *The Economist*. April 18, 2012. http://www.economist.com/node/21560536.

"Chile: Catholics Demand Pope Fire Bishop Complicit in Sex Abuse." *Telesur*. February 7, 2016. http://www.telesurtv.net/english/news/Chile-Catholics-Demand-Pope-Fire-Bishop-Complicit-in-Sex-Abuse-20160207-0036.html.

Cipriano, Ralph. "Lavish Spending Skips the Inner City." *National Catholic Reporter*. June 19, 1998. http://natcath.org/NCR_Online/archives2/1998b/061998/061998a.htm.

Clermont, Betty. "Vatican Corruption, Media Dysfunction, Pope Still the 4th Most Powerful Person in the World." *Daily Kos.* November 22, 2015. https://www.dailykos.com/story/2015/11/22/1452850/-Vatican-Corruption-Media-Dysfunction-Pope-Still-the-4th-Most-Powerful-Person-in-the-World.

Code of Canon Law. Accessed on July 11, 2017. http://www.vatican.va/archive/ENG1104/_P70.HTM.

Coleman, Susan. "Letters." *National Catholic Reporter.* February 10, 2017.

Collins, Marie. "Exclusive: Survivor explains decision to leave Vatican abuse commission." *National Catholic Reporter.* March 1, 2017. https://www.ncronline.org/news/people/exclusive-survivor-explains-decision-leave-vaticans-abuse-commission.

Cooper, Betsy, Daniel Cox, Rachel Lienesch, Robert Jones. "The Rise of the Unaffiliated." *Public Religion Institute.* September 22, 2016.

Cooper, Betsy, Daniel Cox, Rachel Lienesch, and Robert Jones. "Exodus: Why Americans Are Leaving Religion-And Why They're Unlikely To Come Back." *Public Religion Institute.* August 22, 2016.

Coriden, James A. "A Challenge: Making the Rights Real." *Association for the Rights of Catholics in the Church.* Accessed July 19, 2017. http://www.arcc-catholic-rights.net/making_rights_real.htm.

Cox, Stephen. *American Christianity.* Austin: University of Texas Press. 2014.

Craig, Daniel. "Fate of Fishtown church spurs holy war of words." *Philly Voice.* May 5, 2015. http://www.phillyvoice.com/fate-fishtown-church-spurs-holy-war-of-words/.

"Crisis Kit." *Future Church.* Accessed on Jul 11, 2017. https://www.futurechurch.org/save-our-parish-community/save-our-parish-community/resource/crisis-kit.

Day, Donna C. "Church-based Community Organizing: Philadelphia Perspectives." *COMM-ORG.* Accessed on July 18, 2017. https://comm-org.wisc.edu/papers98/warren/faith/day.html.

Dreher, Rod. "Weakland's Exit: A liberal bishop and his downfall." *National Review.* May 24, 2002. http://www.freerepublic.com/focus/news/689151/posts?page=8.

Dick, John Alonzo. *Another Voice: Reflections About Contemporary Christian Belief and Practice.* https://anothervoice-greenleaf.org/.

Dufner, Delores. "Sing a New Church." *OCP*. 1991. https://www.ocp.org/
en-us/products/9922/sing-a-new-church.

Dutch Dominicans. *The Church and the Ministry*. We are Church. Accessed
on July 19, 2017. https://www.we-are-church.org/int/pdfs/KerkEnAmbt/
Kerk_en_ambt-en.pdf.

Eidemiller, Maryann Gogniat. "Closed parishes' sacred goods put to use at
other churches." *OSV Newsweekly*. Accessed on July 18, 2012. https://www.
osv.com/OSVNewsweekly/Story/TabId/2672/ArtMID/13567/ArticleID/2095/
Closed-parishes-sacred-goods-put-to-use-at-other-churches.aspx.

Engel, Justin. "Diocese of Saginaw to reduce services at 53 of 109 churches
across mid-Michigan." *Mlive*. January 20, 2013. http://www.mlive.com/news/
bay-city/index.ssf/2013/01/diocese_of_saginaw_to_reduce_s.html.

English, Bella. "Their Fight Lost, Members of Closed Scituate Church Start
Their Own." *Boston Globe*. October 28, 2016.

"Facts about the Priest Shortage, Optional Celibacy, and Women's
Roles in the Church." *Future Church*. Accessed on July 9, 2017, https://
www.futurechurch.org/future-of-priestly-ministry/optional-celibacy/
facts-about-priest-shortage-optional-celibacy-and.

Feuerherd, Peter. "North Carolina 'Church in Exile' battles restorationists."
National Catholic Reporter. January 26, 2017. https://www.ncronline.org/
blogs/ncr-today/north-carolina-church-exile-battles-restorationists.

"Opponents challenge parish closings, mergers in NY archdiocese." *National
Catholic Reporter*. September 23, 2015. https://www.ncronline.org/news/
faith-parish/opponents-challenge-parish-closings-mergers-ny-archdiocese

Finer, Jonathan. "The Faithful Stand Guard Over Church Near Boston." *The
Washington Post*. September 10, 2004. http://www.washingtonpost.com/wp-
dyn/articles/A9810-2004Sep9.html.

Fittipaldi, Emiliano. *Avarizia*. Feltrinelli Editore. 2015.

Flannery, Tony. "I Am Celebrating a Public Mass on January 22nd: You Are
Welcome to Come if You Wish." Accessed on July 12, 2017. http://www.
tonyflannery.com/i-am-celebrating-a-public-mass-on-january-22nd-you-are-
welcome-to-come-if-you-wish/.

Foss, Michael. *Power Surge; Six Marks of Discipleship For a Changing Church*.
Minneapolis: Fortress Press. 2000.

Fougere, Debora. "Anger Grows at NY Archdiocese for Closing Dozens of Churches." *Al Jazeera*. July 29, 2015. http://america.aljazeera.com/articles/2015/7/29/anger-grows-ny-archdiocese-closing-churches.html.

"Frequently Requested Church Statistics." *Center for Applied Research in the Apostolate*. http://cara.georgetown.edu/frequently-requested-church-statistics/.

Fournier, Deacon Keith. "52 Parishes to Close in the Diocese of Cleveland; Major Restructuring Underway." *Catholic Online*. March 15, 2009. http://www.catholic.org/news/national/story.php?id=32595.

Frogameni, Bill. "The Scum Also Rises." *Scene*. April 4, 2007. https://www.clevescene.com/cleveland/the-scum-always-rises/Content?oid=1498151.

Gay, Malcolm. "Defiant St. Louis Church Wins Archdiocese Suit." *New York Times*. March 17, 2012. http://www.nytimes.com/2012/03/18/us/defiant-st-louis-church-wins-archdiocese-suit.html.

Gabriel, Trip. "Pennsylvania Priest Accused of Abuse Was Reported 5 Years Ago, Records Show." *New York Times*. September 26, 2014. https://www.nytimes.com/2014/09/27/us/priest-in-sexual-abuse-case-was-reported-to-diocese-5-years-ago-records-show.html.

Gavin, Kenneth. "Archdiocese Announces Parish Mergers in Philadelphia as well as Delaware, Montgomery and Bucks Counties Resulting from Pastoral Planning Initiative." *Archdiocese of Philadelphia*. June 1, 2014. http://archphila.org/press%20releases/pr002376.php.

"German archdiocese of Cologne reveals 3.8 Billion dollar fortune." *DailyMail.com*. February 18, 2015. http://www.dailymail.co.uk/wires/ap/article-2958552/German-archdiocese-Cologne-reveals-3-8-billion-fortune.html.

Gibson, David. "Philadelphia Archbishop Chaput welcomes 'smaller church' of holier Catholics." *National Catholic Reporter*. October 21, 2016. https://www.ncronline.org/news/people/philadelphia-archbishop-chaput-welcomes-smaller-church-holier-catholics.

Glatz, Carol. "Archbishop says Vatican officials are 'ashamed to tell people' where they work." *Catholic Herald*. January 15, 2016. http://www.catholicherald.co.uk/news/2016/01/15/archbishop-says-vatican-officials-are-ashamed-to-tell-people-where-they-work/.

Goins-Phillips, Tré. "New study reveals what most Americans believe about female pastors and priests." *The Blaze*. March 15, 2017. http://www.theblaze.

com/news/2017/03/15/new-study-reveals-what-most-americans-believe-about-female-pastors-priests/.

Gray, Mark. "Checkup Time." *1964*. June 8, 2014. http://nineteensixty-four.blogspot.com/2014/07/checkup-time.html.

Grunlund, Maura. "Vatican Appeals could keep Staten Island Roman Catholic churches open." *Silive.com*. January 20, 2014. http://www.silive.com/news/2014/01/hold_for_monday_making_all_thi.html.

Guimaráes, Atila Sinke. "Closing Churches." *Tradition in Action*. January 22, 2004. www.traditioninaction.org. January 22, 2004. http://www.traditioninaction.org/bev/047bev1-22-2004.htm.

"Church Closings in Boston and Solution for Priest Shortage." *Tradition in Action*. October 14, 2004. http://www.traditioninaction.org/bev/058bev10-14-2004.htm.

Hays, Edward. *Prayers for a Planetary Pilgrim*. Notre Dame: Forest of Peace. 2008.

Hickson, Maike. "Pope Emeritus Benedict breaks silence: speaks of deep crisis facing Church post-Vatican II." *Life Site*. March 16, 2016. https://www.lifesitenews.com/news/pope-emeritus-benedict-says-church-is-now-facing-a-two-sided-deep-crisis.

Hildebrandt, Patrick. "New AD Directive is a Call to Arms." *Philadelphia Church Project*. January 11, 2016. http://www.phillychurchproject.com/project-blog/2016/1/10/new-ad-announcement-is-a-call-to-arms.

Hinds, Michael deCourcy. "Schools and Churches Close, Angering Catholics." *New York Times*. Accessed on July 5, 1993. http://www.nytimes.com/1993/07/05/us/schools-and-churches-close-angering-catholics.html.

Holmes, Kristin. "Mergers rip through Conshohocken parishes." *Phily.com*. February 15, 2015. http://www.philly.com/philly/news/pennsylvania/montgomery/20150215_Mergers_rip_through_Conshohocken_parishes.html.

Horowitz, Jason. "Steve Bannon Carries Battle to Another Influential Hub: The Vatican." *The New York Times*. February 7, 2017. https://www.nytimes.com/2017/02/07/world/europe/vatican-steve-bannon-pope-francis.html.

Jungmann, Josef. *The Early Liturgy*. South Bend: University of Notre Dame Press. 1959.

Kirchgaessner, Stephanie, and Amanda Holpuch. "How cardinal disgraced in Boston child abuse scandal found a Vatican haven." *The Guardian*. November 6, 2015. https://www.theguardian.com/world/2015/nov/06/cardinal-bernard-law-disgraced-boston-child-abuse-scandal-vatican-haven-spotlight.

Klauser, Theodor. *A Short History of the Western Liturgy*. New York: Oxford University Press. 1979.

Kuenstler, Sister Kate. "Commentary on Decrees from the Congregation for Clergy Upholding Petition for Recourse Made by Thirteen Parishes of the Cleveland Diocese." *St. Casimir Parish*. Accessed on July 12, 2017. http://www.stcasimir.com/Commentary%20on%20Cleveland%20Decrees%203-29-12.pdf.

Ignatius of Antioch, "Epistle of Ignatius to the Smyrnaeans." *New Advent*. Accessed on July 13, 2017. http://www.newadvent.org/fathers/0109.htm.

Labbe, Mark. "Group says it will end vigil at closed Scituate church." *The Pilot*. May 16, 2016. http://www.thebostonpilot.com/article.asp?ID=176493#.

Landau, Joel, Rikki Reyna, and Reuven Blau. "Catholic Archdiocese of New York to merge 112 parishes into 55 new congregations." *Daily News*. November 3, 2014. http://www.nydailynews.com/new-york/archdiocese-new-york-merge-55-parishes-report-article-1.1996146.

Lindstrom, Natasha. "Reviews imminent for struggling Roman Catholic parishes in Pittsburgh diocese." *Trib Live*. April 26, 2016. http://triblive.com/news/allegheny/10371846-74/parishes-diocese-pittsburgh.

Lipka, Michael. "U.S. Catholics more hopeful than expectant of changes to Church teachings." *Pew Research Center*. March 12, 2014, http://www.pewresearch.org/fact-tank/2014/03/12/u-s-catholics-more-hopeful-than-expectant-of-changes-to-church-teachings/.

Lubano, Alfred. "Anger Over Plans To Sell Church." Philadelphia Inquirer. June 13, 2016. Accessed on July 17, 2017. *Black Christian News Network 1*. http://blackchristiannews.com/2016/06/battle-over-sale-of-phillys-first-black-catholic-church-intensifies/.

Mancini, Roberto. "Vatican's Conspiracy of Silence." *The Guardian*. February 28, 2010. https://www.theguardian.com/commentisfree/belief/2010/feb/28/vatican-ltd-gianluigi-nuzzi.

Marcello, Phillip. "Parishioners Fight AD of Boston for Control of Closed Churches." *Portland Press Herald*. June 10, 2015.

Martos, Joseph. *Deconstructing Sacramental Theology and Reconstructing Catholic Ritual*. Eugene: Wifp and Stock Publishers. 2015.

McClory, Robert. "The Dutch Dominican Plan: Will Innovation Save This Church?" *National Catholic Reporter*. December 14, 2007. http://natcath.org/NCR_Online/archives2/2007d/121407/121407a.htm.

"Hermeneutics as Weapon." *National Catholic Reporter*. August 26, 2011. https://www.ncronline.org/blogs/ncr-today/hermeneutics-weapon.

McElwee, Joshua. "Cardinal Cupich Shoulders Chicago's Future." *National Catholic Reporter*. December 5, 2016. https://www.ncronline.org/news/people/cardinal-cupich-shoulders-chicagos-catholic-future.

"Cardinal Dolan contemplates selling NY chancery in biting letter to priests." *National Catholic Reporter*. January 11, 2017. https://www.ncronline.org/news/vatican/cardinal-dolan-contemplates-selling-ny-chancery-biting-letter-priests.

McGarry, Patsy. "Papal nuncio warns Catholics against becoming 'caricatures.'" *The Irish Times*. August, 22, 2015. https://www.irishtimes.com/news/social-affairs/religion-and-beliefs/papal-nuncio-warns-catholics-against-becoming-caricatures-1.2324952.

McGreevy, John T. *Parish Boundaries*. Chicago: University of Chicago Press. 1996.

Miska, Rhonda. "Q & A with Kate Kuenstler, advising the laity when their parishes face closure." *Global Sisters Report*. November 15, 2016. http://globalsistersreport.org/blog/q/q-sr-kate-kuenstler-advising-laity-when-their-parishes-face-closure-43331.

Morwood, Michael. *Tomorrow's Catholic*. New London: Twenty-Third Publications. 2010.

Murphy, Caryle. "Half of U.S. adults raised Catholic have left the church at some point." *Pew Research Center*. September 15, 2015. http://www.pewresearch.org/fact-tank/2015/09/15/half-of-u-s-adults-raised-catholic-have-left-the-church-at-some-point/.

Musgrave, Jane. "Priest sues diocese, claims it punished him for reporting sex abuse." *Palm Beach Post*. January 11, 2017, http://www.mypalmbeachpost.com/news/crime--law/priest-sues-diocese-claiming-punished-him-for-reporting-sex-abuse/eB6segzLBqLrAwrdpgOxTN/.

Nadeau, Barbie Latza. "Hospital Funds Diverted to Cardinal's Villa." *The Daily Beast.* April 3, 2016. http://www.thedailybeast.com/hospital-funds-diverted-to-cardinals-villa.

"'Monsignor 500' Nunzio Scarano Held in Alleged Vatican Corruption Plot." *The Daily Beast.* June 28, 2013. http://www.thedailybeast.com/monsignor-500-nunzio-scarano-held-in-alleged-vatican-corruption-plot.

A New Vision. *Philadelphia: Catholic Charities Appeal.* 2016. https://www.catholiccharitiesappeal.org/files/5214/5401/8577/CCA_16LeadBrochure.final.pdf.

Nuzzi, Gianluigi. *Merchants in the Temple.* New York: Henry Holt and Co., 2015.

Ohlheiser, Abby. "A Catholic Archbishop Claims He Wasn't Sure Whether Sexual Abuse of Kids Was a Crime." *The Atlantic.* June 10, 2014. https://www.theatlantic.com/national/archive/2014/06/a-catholic-archbishop-claims-he-wasnt-sure-whether-sexual-abuse-of-kids-was-a-crime/372490/.

O'Loughlin, Michael. "Pew Survey: Percentage of US Catholics drops and Catholicism is losing members faster than any denomination." *Crux.* May 12, 2015. http://www.chicagomanualofstyle.org/tools_citationguide.html.

O'Malley, John. W. *What Happened at Vatican II.* Boston: Harvard University Press. 2010.

O'Malley, Michael. "Cleveland Catholic diocese announce church closures." *Cleveland.com.* March 15, 2009. http://blog.cleveland.com/metro/2009/03/parishioners_in_the_cleveland.html.

"Excommunicated Church Thrives Despite Censure." *Huffington Post.* April 17, 2011. http://www.huffingtonpost.com/2011/04/17/excommunicated-church-thr_n_846339.html.

"Parishioners, priest from closed St. Peter Catholic Church defy bishop, celebrate Mass in new home." *The Plain Dealer.* August, 16, 2010. http://blog.cleveland.com/metro/2010/08/parishioners_from_closed_catho.html.

Otterman, Sharon. "Archdiocese of New York Seeks $100 Million Mortgage for Sexual Abuse Fund." *The New York Times.* February 28, 2017. https://www.nytimes.com/2017/02/28/nyregion/archdiocese-sexual-abuse-fund-mortgage.html.

"Feelings of Betrayal after Catholic Church is Leased to Coptic Parish." *New York Times.* March 5, 2017. https://www.nytimes.com/2017/03/05/nyregion/feelings-of-betrayal-after-catholic-church-is-leased-to-coptic-parish.html.

"Heartache for New York's Catholics as Church Closings Are Announced."
New York Times. November 2, 2014. https://www.nytimes.com/2014/11/03/
nyregion/new-york-catholics-are-set-to-learn-fate-of-their-parishes.html.

Pashman, Manya Brachear. "Massive overhaul slated for Chicago Archdiocese." *Chicago Tribune.* February 7, 2016. http://www.chicagotribune.com/
news/ct-archdiocese-parish-reorganization-met-20160205-story.html.

Perkiss, Abigail. *Making Good Neighbors. Civil Rights, Liberalism, and
Integration in Post War Philadelphia.* Ithaca and London: Cornell University
Press. 2014.

Pianigiani, Gaia. "Vatican Finds Stash of Money Tucked Away." *New York
Times.* December 4, 2014. https://www.nytimes.com/2014/12/05/world/
europe/vatican-finds-hundreds-of-millions-of-euros-tucked-away.html.

Pongratz-Lippit, Christa. "Brazil may soon have married
priests, says Leonardo Boff." *National Catholic Reporter.* December 30, 2016. https://www.ncronline.org/news/vatican/
brazil-may-soon-have-married-priests-says-leonardo-boff.

"German priests: open the priesthood to women, make
priestly celibacy optional." *National Catholic Reporter.* January 13, 2017. https://www.ncronline.org/blogs/
german-priests-open-priesthood-women-make-priestly-celibacy-voluntary.

"Pope Francis Discusses Married Priests, Women Deacons with German newspaper." *National Catholic Reporter.*
March 10, 2017. https://www.ncronline.org/news/vatican/
pope-francis-discusses-married-priests-women-deacons-german-newspaper.

Powell, Michael. "At 75, a Battle-Tested but Unwavering Cardinal." *New York
Times.* April 23, 2007, http://www.nytimes.com/2007/04/23/nyregion/23egan.
html.

Provincial and Council of the Dutch Province of the Dominicans. *The Church
and the Ministry.* January, 2007. https://www.we-are-church.org/int/pdfs/
KerkEnAmbt/Kerk_en_ambt-en.pdf.

Pullella, Phillip. "Arrested Vatican Prelate Lived a Lush Life in
Hometown." *Reuters.* July 4, 2013. http://www.reuters.com/article/
us-vatican-bank-investigation-idUSBRE96308S20130704.

"Q & A with Sister Kate Kuenstler." *Global Sisters Report.* November 15, 2016. https://globalsistersreport.org/plus1/vote/
node/43331/plus1_node_vote?token=n9AJlcV7chW06d1QOn877
Gn7-_MjmX0ppZh_GYVtAsQ&destination=node/43331.

"A Report of the Thirty-Seventh Statewide Investigating Grand Jury." *Commonwealth of Pennsylvania, Office of Attorney General.* Accessed on July 19, 2017. http://www.bishop-accountability.org/reports/2016_03_01_Pennsylvania_Grand_Jury_Report_on_Diocese_of_Altoona_Johnstown.pdf.

Roberts, Tom. "Australian priests offer support for deposed bishop." *National Catholic Reporter.* May 3, 2011. https://www.ncronline.org/news/vatican/australian-priests-offer-support-deposed-bishop.

Ruhl, Jack, and Diane Ruhl. "NCR research: Costs of sex abuse crisis to US church underestimated." November 2, 2015. https://www.ncronline.org/news/accountability/ncr-research-costs-sex-abuse-crisis-us-church-underestimated.

Ryan, Michael. "The Second Greatest Scandal in the Church: Priests & Lay Leaders Stealing from the Sunday Collection." *ChurchSecurity.info.* 2003. http://www.churchsecurity.info/Scandal2.pdf.

"The Why & How of Internal Security." *Churchsecurity.info.* Accessed on July 19, 2017. http://www.churchsecurity.info/index_files/Page282.html.

Sanicola, Laura, and Corky Siemaszko. "Locksmiths descend on Our Lady of Peace during its last Mass before the beloved East Side church shutters." *New York Daily News.* August 1, 2015. http://www.nydailynews.com/new-york/locksmiths-descend-lady-peace-mass-article-1.2311109.

Stockman, Dan. "Former LCWR President: Communities must embrace the shift in religious life." *Global Sisters Report.* October 14, 2016. http://globalsistersreport.org/news/trends/former-lcwr-president-communities-must-embrace-shift-religious-life-42726.

"Study of the Impact of Fewer Priests on Pastoral Ministry." *Future Church.* Accessed July 19, 2017. https://www.futurechurch.org/save-our-parish-community/save-our-parish-community/study-of-impact-of-fewer-priests-on-pastoral.

Sweeney, Brigid. "A Catholic Reformation." *Crain's Chicago Business.* July 25, 2016, http://www.chicagobusiness.com/section/catholic.

Taylor, Richard K. "Synod Topical Commission on Moral and Social Issues: Document Comparison of Racism Section." July 24, 2002. Unpublished paper.

Tevlin, Jon. "We're Taking On Water and New Priest Knows He Can't Walk On Water." *Star Tribune.* February 15, 2009.

Tobin, Thomas. "Let's be honest: It's a lack of faith." *National Catholic Reporter.* March 20, 2017. https://www.ncronline.org/blogs/ncr-today/lets-be-honest-its-lack-faith.

Townsend, Tim. "AB Wants St. Stan Priest Defrocked." *St. Louis Post-Dispatch*. January 15, 2008.

"Welcome: About Spiritus." *Spiritus Christi*. Accessed on July 15, 2017. http://www.spirituschristi.org/welcome/about-spiritus/?view=mobile.

West, Melanie. "Manhattan Church Leased to Coptic Catholic Community." *Wall Street Journal*. March 2, 2017. https://www.wsj.com/articles/manhattan-catholic-church-leased-to-coptics-as-community-fights-to-keep-it-1488486322.

Whitman, Gordon, Anne B. Shlay. *Uneven Development*. Philadelphia: Research for Democracy. September 2004.

Willan, Phillip. "How the Vatican Sold Its Soul." *The Guardian*. June 3, 2009. https://www.theguardian.com/commentisfree/belief/2009/jun/03/vatican-central-bank.

Wink, Walter. *Engaging the Powers*. Minneapolis: Fortress Press, 1992.

BIOGRAPHY

Eileen McCafferty DiFranco, M.A. Ed., M.Div. grew up in a working class community in Philadelphia, Pennsylvania and graduated from an integrated all girls' urban Catholic high school. Her early life in her community, school, and church highlighted the problematic influences of racism, sexism, and classism upon both church and society. These early experiences with injustice inspired her and led her to work for gender justice in the Roman Catholic Church and for educational justice for urban public schools where she worked as a school nurse for twenty-five years. A graduate of the Lutheran Theological Seminary of Philadelphia, she was ordained a Roman Catholic Woman Priest in 2006. She remains a community activist while serving as co-pastor of the Community of St. Mary Magdalene, an intentional Eucharistic community in suburban Philadelphia

www.ingramcontent.com/pod-product-compliance
Lightning Source LLC
LaVergne TN
LVHW021453080426
835509LV00018B/2267